PRAISE FOR *MY CUSTOM VAN*

"Like all custom vans, Michael Ian Black's book is customized to fit all your needs and wants for the journey of your life. It's luxurious, entertaining, spooky, disturbing, and hilarious. Devil's in the details! It's stocked with tacos, vampires, squirrels, a cleaning lady, scented candles, salami, tundra, and a foreword by Abe Lincoln himself—now that's Class with a capital C. Enjoy the ride of your lifetime." **—Amy Sedaris**

"This is a great book for shut-ins, for people who like to laugh at sentences, and people who like to move their belongings from place to place. In fact, anyone who likes to pack or ship anything will find a lot to like in these pages." **—Dave Eggers**

"I always walk away jealous and a little fearful of Michael Ian Black's sharp comedic wit. If you like your comedy dry, absurd, and unforced, you will love this book." **—Jim Gaffigan**

MY CUSTOM VAN

And 50 Other Mind-Blowing Essays
That Will Blow Your Mind All Over Your Face

MICHAEL IAN BLACK

SIMON SPOTLIGHT ENTERTAINMENT
New York London Toronto Sydney

SIMON SPOTLIGHT ENTERTAINMENT
A Division of Simon & Schuster, Inc.
1230 Avenue of the Americas
New York, NY 10020

First Simon Spotlight Entertainment trade paperback edition July 2009

SIMON SPOTLIGHT ENTERTAINMENT and colophon are
trademarks of Simon & Schuster, Inc.

For information about special discounts for bulk purchases, please
contact Simon & Schuster Special Sales at 1-866-506-1949 or
business@simonandschuster.com.

The Simon & Schuster Speakers Bureau can bring authors
to your live event. For more information or to book an event
contact the Simon & Schuster Speakers Bureau at
1-866-248-3049 or visit our website at www.simonspeakers.com.

Designed by Nancy Singer

Manufactured in the United States of America

3   5   7   9   10   8   6   4   2

Library of Congress Cataloging-in-Publication Data

Black, Michael Ian.
My custom van / Michael Ian Black.
    p.   cm.
1. American wit and humor. I. Title.
PN6165.B64 2008
818'.602—dc22   2008006725

ISBN 978-1-4169-6405-6
ISBN 978-1-4391-5353-6 (pbk)
ISBN 978-1-4169-6803-0 (ebook)

*For my mother, Jill, who has
always been funny*

Contents

Foreword
by Abraham Lincoln

OF all the conflicts in our nation's history, the Civil War was definitely the shittiest. This terrible war, which was fought sometime in the 1800s, pitted our noble country against itself. North versus South. Brother versus brother. Or a brother and his friend versus a bunch of schoolgirls. I even heard about one instance where a couple of goats fought a set of bagpipes. Dark days indeed.

Most of you probably know that I had the sad honor of being president during that tragic time. As the nation ripped itself apart, I often found myself heavy of heart, and in need of good cheer. In those days we had no television, of course, and so I was forced to take my entertainment from the radio.

This miraculous new invention gave our scarred country much merriment when we needed it most. Many nights, Mary Todd and I would gather our boys around the "talking box," as we called it, and listen to the jesters of the day: Vanderloo P. Vanderloo and his Talking Spinnaker, Haypenny Pete's Rascally Band of Rum Runners, Bob Hope, and so many more.

(Mary Todd was always partial to the humourist Mark Twain, but I think she just liked that bushy mustache of his.

She often remarked how ticklesome it appeared, but she was incoherent much of the time, so I rarely gave her words much credence.)

One evening as Atlanta happily burned to the ground, I heard a new voice come from that talking box. The announcer introduced him as a "fine young comickster, and a good Union boy, even if he is a Jew." Then the young fellow spoke into the amplificator, and what followed was several delightful minutes of amusing patter, quips, and japes, the likes of which I'd never heard before, nor since. I especially recall a mirthful story the man told about eating tacos and the various indigestinal difficulties the foul food produced.

My boy Robert found the man irksome, calling him "an egregious specimen" and "a rapscallion," but one of us was president and one of us was not, so I leave it to the reader to determine who between us had the better sense of humor.

Anyway, by the time this amusing character concluded his tomfoolery, I found myself in such good spirits that I freed the slaves.

Then I grew a beard.

The despondent cloud that hung so heavy upon my countenance was lifted, my merry disposition restored. That night, after I had my way with Mary Todd, I asked her what she thought about inviting this wag to the White House for a command performance. She responded with tears and accusations of the most horrid sort. As I said, though, she was rarely lucid, and in point of fact, several times during our lovemaking called out the name "Jimmy," which I took to be more nonsensical rantings.

The morning next, I instructed my secretary Jimmy to write the man a note, requesting that he make all possible haste to Washington, for I knew his merrymaking would cheer my cabinet and officers as much as it had cheered me. A good Union man, even a Jewy one, would surely do his part for the American cause.

Alas, the performance never occurred. Shortly after dispatching that missive, I was shot in the head by John Wilkes Booth and so never had the opportunity to meet the man who brought me such joy in my time of need—Michael Ian Black.

It was with profound happiness, then, that I received a request to write the foreword for Mr. Black's new book. Reading through an early draft of the anthology, I found myself once again chuckling at his ribald badinage. Yes, thought I, upon reading the selection "A Series of Letters to the First Girl I Ever Fingered," I too have often thought back to the maiden who first felt my manual intrusions. Yes, thought I, reading his comickal gem "Testing the Infinite Monkey Probability Theorem," I too have wondered about the quality of literature three chimpanzees and a bonobo monkey would produce if given several typewriters and a pile of Subway sandwiches. Yes followed yes throughout my perusal of this handsome volume.

Wasn't it me who said, "Without laughter we must cry"? In retrospect that was a foolish thing to say. There are many other things besides crying we might do without laughing: splitting logs, hunting quail, playing Wii, et cetera. Yet the spirit of that humble aphorism holds true. Laughter relieves the tedium of the day; it replenishes the spirit and invigorates the mind. Of course, laughter may also induce the hiccups.

Michael Ian Black's clever new book will, I hope, give all readers much gaiety and few hiccups. (If, by chance, the reader *should* contract hiccups, I find the best cure to be a shot of fresh apple cider vinegar applied through the nose.)

The nation may have paid a dear price for her unity, but it is my hope that this book will do for our nation what no war ever could—create everlasting peace, joy, and love. Is that too much to ask for a book containing an essay entitled "Why I Used a Day-Glo Magic Marker to Color My Dick Yellow"? Perhaps. But I don't think so. And my opinion means more than yours. After all, I was President of the United States of America.

Until I was shot in the head by John Wilkes Booth.

Abraham Lincoln
Springfield, Illinois
2008

What I Would Be Thinking If I Were Billy Joel Driving to a Holiday Party Where I Knew There Was Going to Be a Piano

I'M not doing it. I'm just not. I know I say the same thing every year, but this time I mean it—I am not playing it this year. Seriously, how many times can I possibly be expected to play that stupid song? I bet if you counted the number of times I've played it over the years, it probably adds up to, like, a jillion. I'm not even exaggerating. One *jillion* times. Well, not this year.

This year, I'm just going to say, "Sorry, folks, I'm only playing holiday songs tonight." Yeah, that's a good plan. That's definitely what I'm going to do, and if they don't like it, tough cookies. It'll just be tough cookies for them.

But I know exactly what'll happen. I'll sit down, play a few holiday songs, and then some drunk jerk will yell out "'Piano Man,'" and everybody will start clapping, and I'll look like a real asshole if I don't play it.

I wonder if they'll have shrimp cocktail.

Now that I think of it, it's always Bob Schimke who yells out "'Piano Man.'" He does it every year. He gets a couple of Scotches in that fat gut of his, and then it's "Hey, Billy, play

'Piano Man'!" That guy is such a dick. He thinks he's such a big shot because he manages that stupid hedge fund. Big deal. He thinks because he used to play quarterback for Amherst that everybody should give a shit. I don't. Who cares about you and your stupid hedge fund, Bob? That's what I should say to him this year. I really should. I should just march right up to him and say, "Who cares about your stupid hedge fund?" Let's just see what Mr. Quarterback has to say about that. And I know he made a pass at Christie that time. She probably liked it too.

I'm such a loser.

Why do I even go to these parties? I mean, honestly, how many times do I need to see Trish and Steve and Lily and that creepy doctor husband of hers and all their rich Long Island friends? Although that Greenstein girl is nice. Maybe she'll be there. What's her name—Alison?

What if Alison asks me to play "Piano Man"? Then what? I've got to stick to my guns, that's what. I'll simply say, "Some other time." Yeah, that's good. Kind of like we're making a date or something. And then at the end of the night when we're all getting our coats, I'll turn to her and say something like, "So when do you want to get together and hear 'Piano Man'?" Oh man, that's really good. That's so smooth. After all, how is she going to say no? She's the one who asked to hear it in the first place! Oh man, Billy, that is just perfect.

Maybe she'll say something like, "How about right now?" Yeah. And maybe we'll leave together. I can drive her back to my place and I can play her the stupid song and then maybe we'll do it. I'd really like to do it with that Greenstein girl.

How awesome would that be? Me leaving with Alison on my arm and Bob's big fat stupid face watching us go. That would be too rich. I'd be real nonchalant about it, too—"See you later, Bob."

Who am I kidding? She'd never go out with me. She was dating that actor for a while. What's his name? Benicio? What kind of name is Benicio? A stupid name, that's what kind. Hi, I'm Benicio. I'm so cool. I'm sooooo cool. I should start going by Billicio. I'm Billicio Del Joelio. I play pianolo.

Sing us a song, you're the piano man . . .

Oh great. Now it's in my head. Perfect. Now I have to walk around that stupid party with that stupid song stuck in my head all night.

Amherst sucks at football.

You know what I should do? I should just turn this car around and go home. Just pick up the phone and call them and tell them I ate some bad fish or something. Yeah, that's what I should do.

What am I going to do? Go through my entire life avoiding situations where somebody might ask me to play a song? I can't do that. No, Billy, you've just got to grow yourself a sack and take care of business. And if that loudmouth Bob Schimke requests "Piano Man," I just need to look him in the eye and tell him I'd be happy to play it for him just as soon as he goes ahead and fucks himself.

Who am I kidding? Of course I'm going to play it. I always play it. Probably the only reason half the people at that party even show up is to hear me play "Piano Man." They probably don't even like me. Not really. They just want to tell all their friends that Billy came and played "Piano Man." Again. Like I'm the loser who's *dying* to play it. Whatever.

Fine. I'll do it, but not because *they* want me to, but because *I* want me to. I'm not even going to wait for them to ask. I'm going to march right in there and play the song and that'll be that. I'm not even going to take off my coat first. Yeah. Let's see what Bob has to say about that. I might even play it twice.

One Day, I'm Going to Open a Scented Candle Shoppe

EVERYBODY loves a good scented candle. Scented candles are to people's nostrils what friction is to their genitals—in other words, terrific. Nothing relaxes me more after a stressful day than a stroll through a scented candle shoppe, and I often find myself thinking, *I wonder what it would be like if this store were mine?*

The answer? Wonderful.

One day, I'm going to open a scented candle shoppe. Nothing too fancy. A little gingerbread store just off the beaten path. Someplace travelers will hear about from friends and friends of friends. A special place they'll have to get off the highway to find. They'll drive through some scenic part of the country until they happen upon a local walking along the side of the road. They'll pull their car over and say, "Excuse me, I've heard there's a wonderful scented candle shoppe somewhere around here. Can you point the way?"

The local will give those travelers a little wink and point them in my direction. "Take this road until you come to an old oak tree. Then roll down your windows and just follow the scent of cinnamon until you arrive."

The travelers will thank the old-timer and drive off. (In this scenario the local is an old-timer, but it could just as easily be a freckle-faced paperboy.)

A lot of people may wonder what the difference is between a "shoppe" and a "shop." There's no precise definition, but I'll try to explain. A shop is a place of business. No more. No less. But a shoppe is different. A shoppe is a place where business is conducted, yes, but it's also a place where friendships are formed, trust earned, scented candles smelled.

There's always a dish of free butterscotch candies in a shoppe, and a bowl of milk left out for any stray tabby cats that may wander in. It's a place where Lite FM is always on the radio, except during Christmas, when it's nothing but Nat King Cole and Bing Crosby. A cheerful little bell tinkles when visitors enter, and tinkles again when they go.

"Come again," the owner says, and means it.

"We will," says the customer, and they mean it, too.

A shoppe is a place where if something falls and breaks, the customer offers to pay, but the owner says, "That's all right. The place was getting a little too crowded anyway." Then they both chuckle and eat a butterscotch.

That's the kind of place I'm going to open one day. And it's going to sell scented candles.

What kind of scents? Every kind. Cinnamon, rain forest, pumpkin spice, Drakkar Noir. A Drakkar Noir candle? Yes. Fuck yes.

Of course, a scented candle shoppe needs a name, and I've thought of one for mine. Every good shoppe has a pun in the name, and mine is no exception. I'll call it the Modern Thymes

Scented Candle Shoppe. The sign will be hand-painted in medieval script with a portrait of me dressed as a court jester (a nod to my past as a very famous celebrity), and then underneath there'll be a little slogan: "Smell the difference."

Cute, right?

Inside will be candles. Thousands of candles of all shapes and sizes. Paraffin wax, beeswax, ear wax (just kidding). Votives, tea lights, big candle columns, candles shaped like dragons and wizards. It's going to be great.

Question: When one owns a scented candle shoppe, what does the store smell like? This is a real problem. In the industry, the problem is referred to as STINK (ScenT IngestioN overKill). The problem is, if you have too many scents going at once, they cancel one another out; the nose can only process so much information before it stops being able to distinguish anything. The solution is to choose *one scent* per day. Valentine's Day might be a chocolate-scented day. Halloween might be a chocolate-scented day. I realize I just gave the same example twice, which was a mistake.

Here's an idea I'm presenting to the scented candle national conference when it meets next year in Morrison, Illinois: a "sniffing chamber." This is a separate room within the shoppe for customers who want to sample their scents before purchasing. It's like a tasting spoon for the nose, and I think it has the potential to revolutionize the industry.

Another idea: an American flag candle that smells like victory. I've been to a lot of candle shoppes, and I've never seen a wax representation of "Old Glory." Why not? As I think about it now, I'm realizing it might be because the purpose of candles is to burn them, and some people might object to burning an American flag, even if it is a candle. I still think the smell of victory is a good idea. I don't know exactly what that would smell like. Maybe a combination of burned hair and marshmallows.

Anyway, it's really going to be great. Maybe it'll become a tourist attraction. Maybe I'll even attach a little restaurant, the Thyme Out Café, where people can buy lunch and souvenirs. Like T-shirts that say, "I had a great 'thyme' at the Modern Thymes Scented Candle Shoppe." Or "We had the 'thyme' of our lives at the Modern Thymes Scented Candle Shoppe." That sort of thing.

I've certainly thought enough about it, and I hope one day I will actually get off my duff and do it! Everybody has a dream. Opening an adorable scented candle shoppe is mine.

Of course, the whole thing will be a front for dealing coke.

Maximus Beer

ON behalf of Bob, Donna, and the rest of my team, I want to start this afternoon's presentation with a word of thanks. So Walter, thank you. When I first came to you several years ago and told you that I believed America was ready for a beer that was both low in calories and tasted like somebody's ass, you didn't laugh. Instead, you asked me questions. Good questions, like, "Why would somebody want to drink a beer that tastes like somebody else's ass?"

I didn't have all the answers that day, Walter, but I had a feeling. An unshakable feeling that I was right. So rather than BS you with a bunch of corporate gobbledegook, I just looked you in the eye and said two words. Do you remember what those words were?

"Trust me."

And trust me you did.

We poured millions of dollars into market research. We spent millions more developing the perfect assy taste. And millions more after that, making sure it was the lowest calorie, assiest-tasting beer on the market. And guess what? We did it. It took a hell of a lot of money and a hell of a lot of time, but we did it.

We created "Maximus" beer.

I remember that day when the first focus groups sat down to try it. How nervous we all were. Would they get it? Well, I remember as they took that first drink, they all pretty much said the same thing—those five magic words we'd been waiting years to hear: "It tastes like somebody's ass."

Mission accomplished, Walter. Mission accomplished.

We launched the largest advertising and marketing campaign in this company's history. The ad campaign was brilliant. Supermodels with their backsides facing the camera, all asking the same question: "Does it taste like mine?"

You threw every nickel you had into that campaign. Then you borrowed some more money and threw that in, too. Your Board of Directors said not to do it. They said you were being rash. But you didn't listen. Instead you said to them what I told you so long before.

"Trust me."

In the end, we received a 98 percent saturation rate. Almost one hundred percent of the country knew two things about Maximus—that it was low in calories and that it tasted like somebody's ass.

I'm proud to say that Maximus was the most talked-about product of the year. People talked and talked and talked. Everybody talked about it, from the man on the street to the late-night comics. We were the "butt" of a lot of jokes, Walter, excuse the pun, but we knew who would be having the last laugh, didn't we? Us.

Finally the product launched. After all the research, the ad campaign, the talk, only one question remained: Would they buy it? Would America buy a premium, low-calorie beer that tastes like somebody's ass? We got our answer, didn't we, Walter? We got our answer loud and clear.

No, they would not.

No, they stayed about as far away from a beer that tastes like somebody's ass as they presumably would from somebody's actual ass. It seems in our zeal to perfect Maximus, we failed to answer a simple question—the same question you raised with me, Walter, all those years and all those millions of dollars ago. Why *would* somebody want to drink a beer that tastes like somebody's ass? We finally learned our answer.

They wouldn't.

And when you think about it, why would they? Drinking a beer (even a low-calorie one) that tastes like somebody's ass is essentially the same as just drinking their ass—completely disgusting. Honestly, I'm getting a little nauseated even talking about it.

But you trusted me when I walked into your office, Walter, and for that I am eternally grateful. Especially considering the fact that I was a guy who didn't even finish the eighth grade. A guy who has been convicted multiple times and on numerous counts of public urination. A guy who didn't even work at the company.

A guy who has spent the better part of his life addicted to model airplane glue, and who is, in fact, high on glue right now, which also might explain my nausea.

I started today by thanking you, Walter, and I'd like to conclude by apologizing. I'm sorry. Sorry I bankrupted the company. This family brewery survived for more than two hundred and fifty years before I came along, and then with one bad idea it all went to hell. So that sucks. I'm sorry you lost everything, and I'm really sorry that you hanged yourself. Honestly, I don't even know how your family can afford this nice funeral. All these flowers must have cost a bundle.

Anyway, on behalf of Bob, Donna, and the rest of my team, I'd like to present your wife with this. Sheila, I know this can't possibly make up for all the pain I've caused you and your family, but when you open the envelope, you'll find a coupon good for one free massage every week for a month. To be administered by Bob, Donna, myself, or the rest of my team. Your choice.

Walter, you were a good man.

Why I've Decided to Go Blonde

I'VE been giving this a lot of thought. A LOT of thought. After many sleepless nights, I've decided to go blonde. Believe me, this was not an easy decision. I've spent a lot of time in consultation with my wife and minister (just to clarify, my wife is *not* my minister. They are two different people). We agonized over this decision, we prayed over this decision, and in the end they both told me the same thing: "Follow your heart."

Well, my heart is telling me to give blonde a try.

Is this yet another shallow attempt to save my floundering marriage? Perhaps. After all, my wife always wanted to be married to a blonde man. When we first got together, I led her to believe that I was blonde. Foolishly, she believed me, even though it should have been pretty obvious to her that I was not. For one thing, I have dark hair, which was a real giveaway, but she wanted to believe in me so badly that she allowed herself to be suckered in by my lies. Fourteen-year-old runaways are like that.

Maybe I wanted to believe it, too. For a while there I was even wearing a lot of pastels because I thought they would look good with my blonde hair. But I could only lie to myself for so long. I didn't have blonde hair and for a long time, for years, I thought maybe I never would.

We got married and settled down. Had a couple of kids. Everything was going great. And then I had a relapse. We were at the mall, and a couple walked by. They were about our age. A nice-looking couple. They had their arms around each other and they looked so happy together. But the thing that struck me wasn't so much the way they gazed at each other or the way he was (I thought, inappropriately) licking the inside of her ear. It was his hair. Blonde. Blonde hair cascading down his shoulders into a perfectly coiffed mullet. The kind you sometimes see at drag races and carnivals. I looked at him and thought to myself, *That could be me*.

At first I didn't tell anybody. I was too scared. What if they laughed? What if they rejected me? What if it looked so unnatural on me that I ended up looking like post–plastic surgery Patrick Swayze? After all, I'm a Sephardic Jew. My people have always been swarthy. Swarthy and cheap. For me to turn my back on five thousand years of tradition and go blonde, the thought was incomprehensible. And so I tried to put it out of my mind.

Tried and failed.

I kept envisioning myself looking like that man in the mall. Carefree. Gaunt. Bleeding a little from a cut on the cheek. Blonde. I didn't know what to do. I found myself congregating in places where blonde people hang out. Like Abercrombie & Fitch stores. I rented Robert Redford movies, even though I am against saving the environment. It was a very confusing time. Finally, I couldn't take it anymore. I had to make a decision about my hair.

That's when the sleepless nights started. The thought that kept going through my head was, *How am I going to tell my kids?* I mean, really, how do you look your kids in the eye and tell them that you're going blonde?

My wife and I took them out for pizza and I carefully explained that Daddy was going to change his hair color. Naturally they had a lot of questions, but overall I think they took the news pretty well. Kids are resilient, and the thing that I tried to stress to them was that just because Daddy was going to dye his hair blonde didn't mean I loved them any less. At one point, my son asked, "Is this my fault?" I didn't know whether to cry or smack him across the face. I chose the latter.

Anyway, that's my decision.

What do I hope to gain from this experience? For starters, I want to find out if blondes really do have more fun. Which is to say, do they play more Scrabble?

Also, I think blonde hair will make my cornrows look even better. Yes, they look incredible now. Yes, my dark hair beautifully offsets the tiny white seashells I weave into them. All of that is true. But blonde "Axl Rose style" cornrows would also be off the hook, and if there's one thing I've always wanted to be even more than blonde, it's off the hook.

So there you have it. I've already made an appointment at SuperCuts and I'm not looking back. What my wife and minister helped me realize (again, two totally different people who happened to make me realize the same thing) is that if I don't like my new look, I can always go back to being plain old Michael Ian Black.

But for once, just once, I'd like to be Michael Ian Blonde.

A Series of Letters to a Squirrel

Dear Squirrel,

You're not that cute.

> Sincerely,
> Michael Ian Black

Dear Squirrel,

Hi, it's me again. The "you're not that cute" guy. I feel like I owe you an explanation for that letter I wrote before. You probably felt a little blindsided by it, so I thought I would take a moment to explain what prompted it in the first place.

This morning, I was looking outside my window when I saw you standing on your back legs, nibbling away at a nut you were turning around and around in your two little hands. Turn, turn, turn. Nibble, nibble, nibble. I thought to myself, *I bet that squirrel thinks he is so cute.*

Unwelcome feelings of resentment and jealousy bubbled up inside me. Before I knew it, I was enraged. (Question to self: Who was I *really* angry at? You or me?)

I obviously let my anger get the best of me, and before I knew what I was doing, I hastily wrote that letter and left it at the base of your tree, never considering how potentially hurtful it might be.

Now that I've calmed down, I feel like a real schmuck, so I decided to sit down and attempt to explain my actions. Hence, this letter of apology.

So I'm sorry. I hope you can forgive me, and just know that in the future I will attempt to do a better job controlling my anger rather than letting my anger control me, per my therapist's suggestion.

Sincerely,
Michael Ian Black

Dear Squirrel,

Sorry to bother you AGAIN, but I feel the need to clarify something. In my last letter, I explained why I wrote to you in the first place, and in doing so I think I may have mistakenly left you with the impression that I, in fact, DO think you're that cute. I do not. Nothing could be further from the truth. I do not think you're that cute. I do not think you're cute at all.

My original error was in writing to you to begin with, not in my opinion of your cuteness or lack thereof. My second letter was simply an attempt to explain WHY I wrote the *first* letter, and to apologize for writing it without thinking my actions through. Then, as I said, this *third* letter is to clarify any potential misunderstandings about whether or not I think you are that cute.

Again: I do not.

In fact, I think you look cheap.

Sincerely,
Michael Ian Black

Dear Squirrel,

Now I've gone overboard and I know it. I mean, if my original letter caught you off guard, I can only imagine how that last letter hit you—probably like a ton of bricks. (Although because you are a squirrel, I should probably adjust that expression to something like, "It hit you like a single brick," because the impact of a single brick hitting you would be the rough equivalent of a ton of bricks hitting me.)

Once again, by saying you look cheap, I acted rashly and said something I didn't really mean. After all, how can a squirrel look cheap, anyway? Ha ha.

I don't know if squirrels understand Yiddish, but

now I not only feel like a schmuck but I also feel like a putz. Oy vey.

Sincerely,
Michael Ian Black

P.S. I am leaving a copy of Michael Chabon's wonderful novel *The Yiddish Policemen's Union* as a small token of my contrition. (Another suggestion from my therapist.) Enjoy!

Dear Squirrel,

In my previous letter to you, I asked the rhetorical question, "How can a squirrel look cheap?" Well, I thought about it and I came up with an answer: if the squirrel were wearing too much makeup.

Admittedly, most squirrels do not wear *any* makeup, but it seems to me that if a squirrel did, depending on the amount, it could potentially make the squirrel look cheap.

Clearly you do not wear makeup, and I probably should not have said you look cheap, even though you do. In fact, you look like a whore.

Sincerely,
Michael Ian Black

Dear Squirrel,

By now you are no doubt sick to death of receiving these letters, and I promise this will be the last. The truth is I feel bad about calling you a whore. I don't know anything about your personal life; my judgment was based on nothing more than a general whorish vibe you give off.

You look like you'd screw any squirrel that came your way. You look like you'd even screw the knothole in that tree where you live. But this is all speculation on my part, based on nothing more than your aforementioned whorish vibe and sleazy demeanor. Maybe I'm wrong about you. If so, I apologize.

But I really don't think I am.

Sincerely,
Michael Ian Black

P.S. And you're not that cute.
P.P.S. I notice you haven't even opened the book I gave you. Fuck my therapist and fuck you.

Join Our Club!

GOOD news! Our club is currently seeking a new member. The club does not have a name. It doesn't have a clubhouse. It doesn't even have a permanent address. But it is a *real* club with an *extremely* exclusive membership. How exclusive? We presently number three: myself and the two brothers who own the Chevy Malibu in which we meet.

Maybe you are thinking, *Hey, a club that meets in a less than mint condition 1993 Chevy Malibu doesn't sound like my cup of tea.* Believe me, I understand. If "comfort" and "fun" are high on your list of priorities when joining a fraternal organization, then this may not be the ideal situation for you.

Further devaluing the experience are the facts that neither the radio nor air-conditioning work. On the plus side, the heat works fine, although we often have to keep the windows rolled down in the winter because Randy (the older of the two brothers) suffers from persistent lactose intolerance.

Despite these small inconveniences, the club is a terrific place to unwind with like-minded friends in an intimate and convivial environment.

Perhaps you read the words "Chevy Malibu" and "lactose

intolerance" and think to yourself, *Those guys sound like losers. What possible reason would I have to join?*

If you want a list of reasons, I've got plenty!

For one thing, there is our exhaustive knowledge of all things related to the television program *Babylon 5*. For example, can you name the planet and star system around which Babylon 5 orbits? We can. Epsilon 3 in the Epsilon Eridani star system. No other local fraternal organization can boast this depth of knowledge regarding *Babylon 5*.

Maybe you're looking for a club with social status. If so, consider the fact that Carl (the younger of the two brothers) once made out with 1994 Homecoming Queen nominee Kristi Swinton, and this was BEFORE she put on all that weight! Was there tongue? Yes, there was. I'm not going to regale you with *all* the details because one of the benefits of joining the club is listening to Carl tell the story in person. Teaser: the part where she passes out is a real highlight.

Or maybe you want to join a fraternal organization that gives back to the community. If so, you're in luck. One of the conditions of my probation is that I perform two hundred hours of community service. I checked with my parole officer, and he informed me that anybody is free to assist me as I pick up trash along Route 136. Full disclosure: another condition of my probation is that I stay away from the town swimming pool, so aquatic enthusiasts should take that under advisement.

Maybe you want to join a club with a long history. Our ties go back generations. In fact, Carl and Randy's father and my father used to be in a bowling league together. Further tying us together is the fact that they tag-teamed my mom once.

Another great thing about our club, as compared to some of the ones you may have read about in one of those glossy magazines at the foot doctor, is that our club requires no expensive membership fees. All me and Carl and Randy ask is that, before entering the Malibu, you wipe off your boots because if you don't, mud and gravel get all over the interior. In fact, the only dues you have to pay are gas money and the occasional car wash, which is six bucks. Even though Randy works there, he does not get an employee discount.

We also have our annual "Autumn Solstice" dinner at Shakey's. It would be a nice gesture if you picked up the tab on that, but it is definitely *not* a condition of membership.

Is there a hazing period? Yes, there is. Don't worry, though. Basically, all hazing consists of is us running you through the spanking machine a few times. Honestly, I always feel stupid doing the spanking machine, considering the fact that we are all grown men in our mid- to late thirties, but Carl insists on it. He says that, for him, it's the best part of the club.

Some additional benefits of joining:

- Bi-weekly car rides to Burger King featuring my famous "Burger King Rap." Sample lyric: "I'm gonna purchase two big Whoppers / Then chew them up with my choppers."
- Round Robin seating arrangement.
- Free subscription to Carl's bi-annual *Babylon 5* zine, creatively entitled *Babble On.* Retail value: $11.00
- Free 24/7 access to Randy's DVD collection, which leans

heavily toward sci-fi and Japanese erotic anime. (It's a great benefit, but Randy's late fees are a killer: a hundred dollars per day.)

- Annual Secret Santa gift exchange. Value of gifts not to exceed fifteen dollars.
- Best of all, the pride of obtaining membership in the area's most exclusive club!

If this sounds appealing, feel free to contact me, Head of the Membership Committee, at my mom's house, where I am temporarily residing, or at my place of employment (the address of which I will give when I have a place of employment).

Hey, David Sedaris—Why Don't You Just Go Ahead and Suck It?

FIRST of all, let me start by saying that I am a David Sedaris fan. *Everybody* is a David Sedaris fan, which is part of the reason I hate him so much. People who are as universally beloved as David Sedaris are, in my opinion, highly suspect. After all, how can so many people love you if you are not, on some level, a total shithead?

I would feel much better about David Sedaris if he occasionally threw a telephone at somebody. That's the kind of behavior I have grown accustomed to from the celebrated, and it would greatly relieve me to know that David Sedaris is capable of such lawlessness. A perfect target: fellow memoirist and Nazi hunter Elie Wiesel. How incredible would that be? The winner of the Thurber Prize for American Humor hurls telephone at octogenarian Nobel Laureate. Awesome. Even better, it would provide both of them reams of material for future memoirs. In the business world, we call that "win-win."

But no. Instead, we can expect David Sedaris to continue puttering through his quiet life, trolling Parisian cafés and bookstores, jotting down the occasional bon mot for his adoring American public. All of it so idyllic, so comfortably bohemian. So fucking perfect. Which is why I say:

Hey, David Sedaris—why don't you just go ahead and suck it?

Geniuses are the worst. If you are at all like me, you believe that geniuses were put on this earth to rub your nose in the stink of your own mediocrity. Honestly, is humanity really served by geniuses? Yes, they contribute to the arts and sciences, but ultimately, don't they take far more than they give? By simply existing, aren't they robbing the rest of us of the illusion of our potential greatness? Sedaris writes bestselling book after book, which only goes to prove time and time again that he is capable of greatness and you are not. If that doesn't make you feel bad about yourself, it should.

Perhaps you think my antipathy is based on nothing more than good old-fashioned jealousy. You would be right to think this. After all, David Sedaris is living the kind of sophisticated, glittering life I always envisioned for myself, minus the homosexuality. So how come good fortune fell his way, and not mine? After all, we have so much in common. I too grew up in a highly dysfunctional family. I too have kept a diary my entire life (although I prefer the word "journal," because mine is bound in human skin). I too worked as a housecleaner (not true) and a Macy's elf (also not true). So, given all these amazing similarities, how is it that David Sedaris is winning various literary honors and I am doing commercials for Sierra Mist? Which is why I say again:

Hey, David Sedaris—why don't you just go ahead and suck it?

It's important to understand that when you read the words "David Sedaris" and "suck it," that they are not *actually* directed at David Sedaris the person, but more at *the idea* of David Sedaris—the idea of a diminutive comedic memoirist out there selling millions of books and living in Paris with his boyfriend, Hugh. Now, perhaps the idea of David Sedaris coincides pretty closely with the actual David Sedaris, but only because he's leading a *very specific* kind of life that I feel is designed to make people think worse of me. Is this narcissistic? On his part, yes.

Lest you think I only feel this way about David Sedaris, I don't. Wes Anderson, you can go ahead and suck it, too. And so can you, Jonathan Safran Foer. I'd love to go to a dinner party with all of those guys and listen to them talk about how great they are. Except they wouldn't. They would probably be humble and complimentary of everybody else. Chances are, nobody would even throw a telephone at anybody, unless it was me throwing the phone, which I would do out of frustration and self-loathing. Who would I throw it at? Myself.

(Can you throw a telephone at yourself? I suppose you could if you used the cord as a kind of bungee cord and whipped the receiver against your forehead. That's probably what I would do, and in a few years, I would find the incident relayed in one of their books or movies, only it would be painted in much more vivid colors than what actually took place.)

I hope that David Sedaris is, on some level, a total shithead. Otherwise, I would have a hard time claiming him for humanity. Because in the end, aren't we all shitheads, even the geniuses among us? I like to think so. But just in case he isn't, let me say for the final time:

Hey, David Sedaris—why don't you just go ahead and suck it?

Erotic Fiction: The Elevator

From time to time, I like to dabble in erotic fiction. I do this because I am a romantic at heart, and because it gets me off. Enjoy . . .

YOU'RE in an elevator with a pretty girl. As the doors close, you both reach for the same button. When you do, your fingers brush against each other. A graze, no more. She smiles, embarrassed, and looks away. Well, well, looks like you're heading to the same floor. A shared destination. Kismet?

The two of you are alone. As the elevator begins its ascent, your mind races. Stealing glances at her from the corner of your eye, you wonder how to speak to this delectable creature. What can you say to bewitch her as much as she has enchanted you? The words, when they come, are perfect. "Same floor, huh?"

A breath. The scent of lilacs as she turns to you. Her response fills you with delight. "Huh?" she says.

You waggle your freshly waxed eyebrows at her and nod mischievously toward the elevator wall. "Same floor. You and me."

Her dappled eyes go to the button, the only button lit, and she says, "I guess."

"Indeed," you say with confidence. You have made contact. It is now only a matter of time before your bodies are entwined in divine rapture, perhaps in this very elevator, or perhaps in some dim alcove on the floor above. The floor that the two of you share. The floor that you race toward even now.

A breath. No more than a breath before she turns to you and says, "There are only two floors."

And so there are. She is magnificent. Beautiful and brilliant. From what star did this golden light first emerge? Across what vast distance did it travel to find you here?

She continues, "So obviously we're going to the same floor."

But angels were not meant to be captured so easily. She clearly likes the chase. And so, chase you shall: "It wasn't obvious to me," you say, as you let the tiniest dribble of tobacco juice slide out of your mouth—just enough so that it catches the light dripping into your plastic dip cup.

"Listen, asshole," she says, "this hospital only has two floors. The ground floor, and upstairs where I get my fucking chemotherapy."

She starts crying. And coughing.

You ride the rest of the way in silence. It is a very slow elevator.

A College Application Essay to Harvard That Might Have Been Written by a High School Senior Who Has Absolutely No Chance of Getting Accepted

FROM the 2007 "Common Application" for admission to Harvard College:

> "Discuss some issue of personal, local, national, or international concern and its importance to you."

In this essay I am going to discuss war. I believe that war is terrible, even in Africa. For example, have you heard about the situation in Darfur? Darfur is a territory in the country of Sudan. According to the Internet website Wikipedia, between 200,000 and 400,000 people have been killed in Darfur. If that doesn't make your heart truly ache, perhaps nothing will. Not even homeless people. It is truly terrible. But the worst part is that the world does not seem to care. Nobody is doing anything about this deplorable and egregious situation. Not even Bono.

Sometimes I just want to scream, "WHY???" because this terrible war is so futile and inefficacious. But what can one teenager do to stop the madness which is the killing in Darfur in the country of Sudan? Sadly, the inescapable conclusion I am drawn to, as if a moth to a flame, is, not much. Yes, it seems as though one teenager can do so little, no matter how many extracurricular activities he or she has.

Why isn't the president, George W. Bush, doing anything to stop this carnage and mayhem which the world knows as Darfur? Were I president, the first thing I would do would be to call together all of the other presidents and kings from around the world and assemble them within the confines of the White House. Then, after a fancy meal and a performance by the country duo Brooks & Dunn, I would get "down to business."

I would say, "Listen to me. This intolerable war in Darfur in the country of Sudan has to stop! We are all leaders of this world, the only world we have, and we must put an end to it!"

Why is this issue personally important to me? Because I believe that war is wrong. People should not be fighting each other. I personally do not want to fight in wars, nor do I want others to fight in them, especially the precious children. No precious child should ever have to fight in wars, nor die in them. Instead, children should be free to play and ruminate upon their futures without fear of being killed by war.

My grandmother died after contracting a deadly form of cancer. As I stood there that day, holding her withered hand and contemplating my reflection reflected back to me in her cloudy eyes, I truly understood what it means to lose somebody dear.

If I get accepted to Harvard, I will devote myself to the noble cause of world peace. I plan on majoring in International

Relationships, with a minor in Theater. Second, I want to use my degree to make the world a better place so that there will never be any more wars. Perhaps you will think I am naïve, just another optimistic teenager who believes he can change the world. So be it. If that is the case, I say, "Just watch me achieve my goals!"

Yes, I may be just a "teenager." And I may be "young," but I truly believe that it is the youth of this country, the United States of America, who will someday change the world. Not just by raising money at rock concerts featuring the hottest bands. Nor by simply donating canned goods to the needy, but by actually participating in such global events as the Darfur Conflict in the Darfur region of the African nation Sudan.

As a former president of our nation, John Fitzgerald Kennedy, once intoned, "Ask not what your country can do for you, but what you can do for your country." I believe that I have truly taken these words to my heart. Furthermore, I believe that Harvard College will actually teach me to apply this great president's words to my own life, through my studies in International Relationships and Theater.

After I graduate from Harvard (fingers crossed), I am going to join the Peace Corps and devote myself to helping the poor suffering African people and their precious children. How? By digging wells, giving malaria shots, and teaching them to play the mandolin, which I currently study. Just imagine if one person can do this, what lots and lots of people joined together could do if only we listened to the late singer John Lennon, who sang "Give Peace a Chance" before he was gunned down in front of his apartment building by Mark David Chapman in 1980.

Yes, I believe that "giving peace a chance" is the only way to stop wars. Also, global warming is terrible.

Taco Party

GUESS what? I'm having a taco party, and you're fucking invited. It's going to be the greatest fucking taco party ever. I'm gonna have every kind of fucking taco imaginable. Hard shell! Soft shell! Hell's bells! This is going to be the wickedest fucking kick-ass taco party on EARTH!

And everybody's fucking invited! You're invited! That fucker over there is invited! All you fuckers are fucking invited to come on over and eat some truly sick, mouthwatering fucking tacos at the greatest fucking taco party extravaganza ever!

CHICKEN! BEEF! FISH! PORK! GRILLED VEGGIES? FUCK YES!

Plus so much *carne asada* you'll be fucking begging for mercy!

Here's the way the day breaks down: Fucking show up at noon. Eat fucking tacos until you either boot or pass the fuck out or both. That's it. If you want, you can take a couple swipes at the fucking piñata I got specially made in the shape of a taco. What's it filled with? You guessed it, fucker. Tacos. I got a fucking taco-shaped piñata filled with fucking tacos!!! How fucking sick is that? It's like the fucking *Matrix*, only with tacos instead of Keanu Reeves.

You want to swim? You can fucking swim all you want. Guess what the pool is filled with? Did you fucking guess guacamole? Wrong, fucker. It's filled with water because YOU CAN'T FUCKING SWIM IN GUACAMOLE!!! We tried that last year and it didn't fucking work. The pool is filled with water. So if you want to swim, bring your trunks and fucking go crazy. One rule, though: no taco farts in the pool! If you fucking cut a taco fart in the pool, I swear to God, I will be really fucking pissed.

Will there be entertainment? Fuck yes! For this year's festivities I will be serving as DJ, spinning a steady, unceasing diet of AC fucking DC on my vintage 2002 5GB iPod because AC/DC goes with tacos the way Mike Nichols goes with Elaine fucking May!

This is going to be the taco party to end all fucking taco parties. Maybe you like olives on your tacos. Guess what, fuckwad? I will have olives. Maybe you like chopped green onion drizzled in olive oil. Hey, fucking dicknose ass-cheeks shithead—I WILL HAVE CHOPPED GREEN ONIONS DRIZZLED IN OLIVE OIL!!! I will have every conceivable taco topping, including some very fucking exotic habanero peppers I specifically imported from your mother's ass!

It's going to be ridicufuckinglous.

So, let's party. Party some more. Continue fucking partying. Then, as the sun sets, I'm going to break out the sparklers and go fucking CRAZY! There are unlimited sparklers for whoever wants, courtesy of my cousin Richie, who lives in Kentucky, where all they fucking do is light off sparklers.

This is going to be the ultimate fucking taco party/swimming party/sparkler fuckfest.

DO NOT PUT THE FUCKING SPARKLERS IN THE POOL!!!

If I find any fucking sparklers in the pool, I am taking away the sparklers. I am not kidding. I will have a zero fucking tolerance policy when it comes to sparklers and/or taco farts in the pool. Let this serve as your warning because I don't want anybody bitching at me that they didn't get warned about this. I am fucking warning you now and I will not brook any fucking objections.

This is going to be the sickest fucking taco party EVER! We did this party last year and it was radical! How radical? My buddy Greg fucking died! That's how fucking awesome it was. This year, I'm hoping two fucking fuckers die! How incredible would that be?

If they have to drag some of you fucking fuckers out of here in body bags, I will be so fucking stoked.

Fair warning: If you don't like AC/DC, stuffing your fat face full of tacos, playing fucking taco piñata, swimming in crystal-clear, taco fart–free waters, and waving around fucking Kentucky bluegrass sparklers, then stay home and suck on your grandma's fucking tit, because this is not the fucking party for you.

On the other hand, if this sounds as truly twisted to you as it does to me, then without question this is going to be the single most important party of your entire fucking life. But be prepared for the long haul, because we are going to party as long as the tacos and the sparklers hold out, or until the fucking cops shut us down, or until seven-thirty, which is when I told my mom I would clear everybody out.

By the way, it's BYOFB, fucker.

Vampires—Good for the Economy?

WITH oil prices spiking, interest rates rising, and consumer confidence depressed, it might be time to finally consider how the sudden emergence of a vampire army would affect the American economy. My team of graduate students and I have spent the past several months poring over data and creating complex computer models in order to determine the answer to this vitally important question.

Our findings were startling. Contrary to conventional wisdom, we now believe that a small- to moderate-sized horde of vampires would actually be *good* for the economy. Why? Let's begin by looking at some industries that would immediately benefit from an onslaught of bloodthirsty, rampaging vampires.

- Cape manufacturers. For the last hundred and fifty years or so, the cape industry has been on a slow and steady downward trajectory. We believe that even a few thousand ravenous vampires could reverse this entire sector's fortunes, as vampires seek to outfit themselves in the latest capery. Impact on nonvampire fashion could also be substantial: look for velvet, silk, and corset sales to rise.

- Garlic farmers. Even though the FDA has never proven the efficacy of garlic in warding off vampires (or even tested it), old wives' tales die hard. In the event of vampire attack, per household garlic consumption will triple, or even quadruple. Look for entrepreneurs to capitalize: garlic toothpaste, garlic milk, and garlic-polyester blends may all become commonplace.
- Coffin makers. Vampires will need a place to sleep during daylight. Plus, they will be killing people. These two factors will combine to make the coffin industry a profitable one indeed.
- Angry villagers. While technically not an "industry," angry villagers have traditionally responded aggressively to ravenous legions of the undead. These villagers will need torches, spikes, crosses, and bullhorns. Expect minimal but appreciable gains in these commodity suppliers.

As in any economic shake-up, some businesses will suffer. Look for the following manufacturers to take the biggest hits:

- Makers of fake plastic and wax vampire teeth. While only a small part of the overall novelty industry, makers of fake plastic and wax vampire teeth will likely suffer the same fate that makers of realistic toy guns experienced during the crack cocaine epidemic of the 1980s and '90s. Aggressive policing and mistaken identities will put fake vampire teeth manufacturers under tremendous pressure.
- Travel and tourism. While pandemics are generally bad for the tourism industry, the variables related to a vampire at-

tack remain too disparate to predict, and thus, while travel and tourism will certainly suffer, it is an open question as to how much. One potential upside: if the undead can be contained, it is possible that some form of tourism might actually *improve* in vampire "hot zones," creating opportunities for so-called "adventure tourism" outfits that will specialize in observing, and even hunting, vampires.

Some other findings:

Although vampires do not kill based on socioeconomic status, we expect the poor to be disproportionately affected, since they will be the least able to protect themselves, as well as the most likely to be wandering outside alone at night. We are calling this phenomena "the vampire tax." Look for Democrats to capitalize.

There could be an unintended benefit from this "vampire tax." Because the most likely vampire victims are the same people most likely to use social services, there is a possibility that social welfare programs may actually begin to shrink, as their clientele is slaughtered by marauding bands of soulless wraiths. Savings to the nation could be substantial.

The stock market, of course, will suffer enormous short-term losses in the immediate weeks and months following the arrival of thousands of undead sucking the life force from the citizenry. Patience, though, will make this temporary correction a glittering opportunity for the shrewd investor.

In conclusion, we are confident that long-term benefits will offset any short-term losses resultant from a vampire invasion. Within two years, we believe the economy will not only fully recover to pre-vampire levels, but may actually thrive. In short, vampires would be good for the economy.

Zombies, on the other hand, would be a fucking disaster.

Grasshopper

UPON waking this morning, I discovered a grasshopper in my bed. The grasshopper was larger than average, and dressed in a little suit. Also, amazingly, it talked. Needless to say, I was very surprised. Unfortunately, the grasshopper spoke French, which I do not speak. Consequently, I did not think twice before killing it with my shoe.

In retrospect, I wonder if this was a mistake. My wife speaks fluent French, and it would have been no big deal to go downstairs and ask her to come up and translate. Perhaps the grasshopper had words of great wisdom to share. If not, I still could have killed it with my shoe.

Perhaps you think I am a cruel man. Maybe you are thinking the grasshopper did nothing to deserve its fate. But let me ask you: What do *you* do when you find a large insect in bed with you? Kill it, right? Right.

Perhaps you are thinking, *Yes, but this grasshopper spoke French*. So what? I admit it is unusual, but just because something speaks French doesn't mean you shouldn't kill it. Look at Marie Antoinette. She spoke French. Did that fact prevent the citizenry from chopping off her head? No it did not.

The only thing I regret about the whole incident was that I wasn't able to save the grasshopper's little suit. It seemed very stylish, and afterward I noticed that it was from Club Monaco, which is a good store. I really should have saved that suit. But, as the French say, *"c'est la vie."*

The Complete Idiot's Guide to Meeting People More Famous Than You

A scenario: you are gamboling along the promenade when you spot your favorite celebrity enjoying a gelato. You stop in your tracks, jaw agape. You have often felt that you and this celebrity would become fast friends were you ever to meet; now, finally, is your opportunity.

What to do? How best to approach? Casually? With vigor? Should you "accidentally" spill your Big Gulp on his sweater? Discreetly cup his buttocks? Sweat begins to pool in your unmentionables. You are as frozen as that gelato your favorite celebrity passionately licks, as you yourself would like to be licked. What are you supposed to do? Don't worry. I am going to help you. As a celebrity myself (very famous), I have often heard other celebrities talk about "giving back to the community," and that's great for them. I'm told volunteering for stuff is a terrific way to get laid. While I have no interest in donating time or money to "causes," I would like to give something back to the little people who have made me so very popular on basic cable.

It is in that spirit that I offer these simple tips for approaching tremendous stars like myself:

First of all, relax. Famous people are just like you. Yes, we have more money. Yes, we are invited to parties so fabulous your head would explode were you ever to get past the velvet ropes. But after the flashbulbs have stopped popping and we roll out of bed around noon, we are just like you—we have people who put our pants on us one leg at a time.

Approach a celebrity the way you would an old friend. An old friend who doesn't remember you. Just walk up, extend your hand, and give a hearty, "Ahoy!" Everybody enjoys a familial naval greeting, especially stars. If you have the time to doff naval dress whites, all the better.

Next, have a plan in mind. Many people are so happy just to be in the presence of the famous that they become completely tongue-tied once they've achieved this goal. Not you. You will know what you want to say and you will say it. For example, when approaching John Travolta, you might say, "Ahoy, John. I'm a big fan. Is it true you're gay?" Then, the two of you can have a long and meaningful discussion about his sexuality. The next thing you know, he's jetting off with you to meet Kelly and the kids in his private 747, while whispering the secrets to getting past the infamous Xenu's Wall of Fire level in your Scientology training. All because you had a plan.

Maybe you want an autograph. Most stars are happy to oblige. A word to the wise, however: have your pen at the ready. Nothing is more awkward than spending long minutes fishing through your purse trying to find something to write with, only to emerge with a melty lipstick. It's awkward and it makes you look cheap. If you don't have a pen, remember that God gave you natural ink—your own blood.

Pay that person a compliment, but don't kiss their ass. For example, one time I saw Cameron Diaz at a party and told her I thought she was pretty funny for a girl. She was very flattered because she understood that I respected her enough to not insult her intelligence by saying she was as funny as a man. Long story short: I banged her.

Also, don't be afraid to offer money. Think about all the enjoyment that person has given you over the years. Would it kill you to approach with a twenty-dollar bill in hand? Some celebs will take checks. Personally, I walk around with one of those slidy doodads for imprinting credit cards. Sure it's heavy, but I do it. Why? Because I care about the fans.

Finally, know how to make a graceful exit. You've met that big star, gotten an autograph. Maybe the two of you made out a little. Great. Now it's time to go. Yes, there will be tears. Some hurtful words might be exchanged, but that's just because love can be so painful. Causing a scene will only make it harder for both of you to let go. A quick hug, and then it's back to your separate lives. You, to your humdrum workaday world, the star back to his gated community, opulent lifestyle, and prescription narcotics.

It doesn't seem fair, does it? Of course not. And yet, that's just the natural order of things. Some people are famous and some are not. It doesn't mean one person is better than the other.

I'm just kidding. That's exactly what it means.

My Custom Van

THE minivan killed America. Consider the country pre-minivan: muscular, fiercely independent, sex-loving. Consider the country now: atrophied, communal, prudish.

Why did vans need to shrink? They were perfect the way they were. Big, bad, endlessly customizable. What was once the ultimate pussymobile suddenly downshifted into a bland, proletarian motor vehicle. Why? The A-Team didn't ride in a minivan. SWAT teams don't pour out the back of minivans. The only teams that emerge from minivans are kids' soccer teams, and kids' soccer teams don't kick ass. They kick soccer balls.

We were Americans once. Meat eating, beer swilling, unfiltered cigarette–smoking Americans who drove vans and kicked ass. What are we now? Pantywaists and sissies. We used to be Americans, damn it. Now we're global citizens.

Fuck that. I'm getting a van.

Moreover, my van is going to be awesome. After all, there's no point in getting a van if it *isn't* going to be awesome. To express this thought mathematically: Custom Van = Awesome.

What makes a custom van awesome? It starts with the paint job. A van's paint job should say something about its owner. It should attempt to embody the owner's highest aspirations for himself. It should be a visual representation of his ethos, his creed. But it should also feature a naked chick on a horse. For example, an awesome custom van might depict an airbrushed naked chick riding a horse right into a dick. That would be pretty cool.

But my sensibility is somewhat more refined, and my van's paint job will reflect that. Which is why I've decided my van is going to feature a wizard flying atop the winged horse Pegasus, staff in hand, casting wicked laser lightning bolts below. Where's the naked chick? I'll give you a second to figure it out.

Did you get it? The wizard IS the naked chick! How radical is that? Answer: a million. It's a million radical. While the picture itself will be incredible, it is also loaded with symbolism. The wizard represents ambition and magic. The laser lightning represents power. The Pegasus represents a cool horse, and the fact that the wizard is actually a naked chick represents both my verdant sexuality and my verdant awesomeness.

(And for you English majors who are going to say, "He's using the word 'verdant' wrong," guess what? I know what verdant means and I'm using it exactly right, which speaks further to my verdant awesomeness.)

I should probably add that the van's base color is going to be deep blue, to further enhance the illusion that the wizard chick is flying through the upper reaches of the atmosphere, which is not only outer spacey but also implies coldness, which of course necessitates that her nipples be hard.

That's the exterior.

The challenge, then, is to make the inside as awesome as the outside. When decorating an interior, I like to go with a "classic contemporary" motif. This means honoring the past without a slavish devotion to the stale conventions of yester-year.

How's this for starters? Instead of decorating with the tra-ditional shag rug, I am going to go with flokati, which looks exactly like shag, but is a lot more expensive. That way, when I've got a lady back there and she asks, "Is that shag?" I can answer, "No, baby, that's flokati." When she asks what the dif-ference is, I won't directly answer. Instead I'll rub my thumb and middle finger together in the international sign of "very pricey."

Historically, wood paneling is chosen for a custom van's interior walls. Not so in my case. I'm going to go with bamboo. Just as tough as wood, but environmentally friendly. Sustain-able, just like the huge boner I'm going to get when my lady friend and I run our hands along its smooth surface. "Bam-boo," I'm going to whisper in her ear.

Do you hear that? That's the small, soft sound of her pant-ies hitting flokati.

Then there are the small details that will raise the tem-perature from merely awesome to Simply Awesome. The steering wheel, for example. How to wrap it? Rich wood ve-neer, leather, aluminum? No. Because there's not going to be a steering wheel. Instead, I'm going to control the van with a vintage Atari 2600 joystick. How radical is that? Again, a million radical. Of course, the fire button on the joystick will not actually fire anything, but it *will* make laser sound effects, a subtle reminder of the laser lightning featured so prominently outside.

Here's the coup de grâce: fudge cabinet. That's right. I'm going to build a small pullout drawer that will house nothing but fudge. Imagine me and my lady sprawled out in the back, wrapped in nothing but a cashmere spread. We are postcoital and feeling peckish. I casually lean over and pull open a mahogany drawer. Inside are individually labeled chunks of handmade fudge, accumulated from the various mom-and-pop fudge shops I passed along my journeys. Check and mate.

Then there's the license plate. Obviously I'm going to need to go custom with the plates. I have a few ideas.

- Wkd Wzrd (Wicked Wizard)
- AwsmWzrd (Awesome Wizard)
- WzdfOzm (Wizard of Oz-some)
- PsseMbl (Pussymobile)
- Lzr Sdz (Laser Sounds)
- Flokati (Flokati)
- Dlbrt (Dilbert—because I'm a fan)

What's the total price tag on a custom van this awesome? I figure I can do the whole thing (including fudge) for around $100,000. Can I afford to spend that kind of money on a purely discretionary purchase like a custom van? Let me answer that question with a question: Can I afford *not* to? Now let me answer the question I posed to answer the first question: No.

MY CUSTOM VAN

No, I cannot afford not to. Yeah, that's a triple negative. Which is not only fantastically syntactic ("syntastic"), it is yet another example of my verdant awesomeness.

I am the wizard. The wizard is I.

A Meditation on Salami

TANGIER than bologna, rounder than ham, exoticker than turkey, salami has never gotten its proper due. Which is sad, considering that salami IS THE GREATEST LUNCH MEAT IN THE WORLD! If I seem a little overenthusiastic, it is perhaps because salami has so many detractors. Why? For starters, the name: salami. It sounds stupid, like a reject from the Seven Dwarfs. Sleepy, Grumpy, Salami.

Or like an acronym for something else. SaLAMI: Sandwich Lovers All Make It. That's a terrible example of what the acronym for salami could be, but I think you get my point.

Also, salami seems to awaken the xenophobia in people. It's kind of Italian, but kind of New Yorky (Jewish), and it seems like exactly the kind of food that terrorists might enjoy. One could easily imagine a group of bearded cave dwellers gnawing on hunks of salami while plotting the demise of the Great Satan. Of course, one could also easily imagine that same group juggling bowling balls on the moon, for the simple reason that imagining stuff is easy.

(A quick note: I'm not ascribing any superhuman juggling abilities to terrorists. Far from it. If anything, juggling bowling balls on the moon would be considerably easier than here on Earth, due to the moon's lower gravity. Besides, terrorists probably hate juggling, because juggling is one of our freedoms.)

Probably the biggest modern objection to salami is that it falls into that category of foods made from the leftover parts of other foods. A piece of salami, mottled in various attractive shades of pink and white, is like some kind of Frankenstein creation: a little beef, a little pork, and a lot of other stuff. Horse lips, for example.

Well, if salami is merely a hodgepodge concoction from whatever is left on the slaughterhouse floor, then give me a broom and tell me where to start sweeping, because salami, for all its faults, is delicious: salty, greasy, and just the right amount of chewy. It's no wonder that the word "salami" is also informally used in baseball circles to describe a grand-slam home run. It's just that good. What other lunch meat can make that claim? Never will liverwurst be used to describe anything other than liverwurst.

And salami is versatile. Yes, it's a sandwich staple. But it's also great with scrambled eggs. And fabulous on pizza. How about as the foundation for a killer antipasto salad? Or simply rolled up and savored with my favorite: a tall, room-temperature bottle of Bud Light!

Also, salami doesn't spoil like other luncheon meats. Try leaving a pound of ham outside on a hot day for a few hours. See what happens. Actually, I'll tell you so you don't waste food: it goes bad. Salami just gets more delicious. And more warm.

Some people think salami is bad for you. Yes, it's high in

the kind of fat that gives people heart attacks, but I compared the life expectancy of Italians versus the life expectancy of United States of Americans. Guess what I discovered? Italians live longer! Why? Because salami is literally the only thing they eat over there!!!

(Another quick note: We both know that Italians eat other foods besides salami, but I felt like it was okay to use a little "dramatic license" here. For the record, Italians also eat spaghetti and cannoli.)

Now I know salami isn't "cool." "Cool" people like that pretty girl from *Boston Legal* aren't sitting around on their yachts in Beverly Hills snacking on salami. So what? Being a celebrity myself (very famous), I know a lot of those so-called "cool" people, and let me tell you something: a lot of them are very unhappy. Is there a correlation between their unhappiness and the lack of salami in their diets? I'm not saying yes. On the other hand, I am most decidedly not saying no.

All I'm asking is that the next time you find yourself brown-paper-bagging it, you give salami another look. Maybe you'll walk away from the experience with a shrug. So be it. But maybe, just maybe, you'll finish up that lunch with a smile on your face, the kind of smile that announces to the world, "Either I just ate a salami sandwich or else I'm wearing a little too much lip gloss."

Now We Will Join Forces, You and I

NOW we will join forces, you and I. We will make sandwiches. The kinds of sandwiches that only two forceful people can make: ham AND cheese, bologna AND cheese, peanut butter AND cheese. We will pack these sandwiches into a wicker picnic hamper and carry them to the top of a hill. The hilltop upon which we eat our forceful sandwiches will overlook a carnival, created by us. We will call this carnival the Carnival of the Festive Raccoons!

There will be no actual raccoons at this carnival.

But there will be prizes. Yes, we will supply prizes, you and I. Big inflatable frogs, plastic key chains, noisemakers, enormous stuffed animals not in the shape of raccoons. And there will be games. Many games. Games of skill. Games of chance. Games that will be rigged so that nobody wins.

It will be an excellent celebration. We will eat our sandwiches and watch the townspeople enjoy this carnival honoring raccoons. We will delight in their confusion as children turn to their parents and ask, "Where are all the raccoons?" We will watch as the parents turn this way and that searching for raccoons.

Again, there will be no raccoons at this carnival.

We will sit atop that hill and watch the carnivalgoers, you and I. But they will be unable to see us watching them, unless they have night-vision binoculars, which will be very unlikely because we will employ security guards to frisk people for night-vision binoculars as they enter the carnival grounds. Our privacy will be of paramount importance.

THE RIDES WILL NOT REQUIRE ANY TICKETS!!!

Yes, carnivalgoers will be able to board any ride at will, regardless of height or heart condition. Pregnant women will be allowed to ride the loop-dee-loop and other nausea-inducing attractions. Even small children will be permitted to go on whatever ride they desire. It will be very unsafe. But we will not care.

We will join forces in not caring, you and I. We will eat our forceful sandwiches and watch the small, pregnant carnivalgoers injure themselves and we will say to each other, "That's what happens when you allow the free market to run amok." We will not know what it means when we say it, but we will laugh anyway. We will join forces in not understanding our own witticisms.

The night will be long and cold. We will bring blankets and a thermos filled with hot cocoa. We will pass the hot cocoa back and forth, not caring that we may get each other's germs. We will join forces in not caring about germs or the fact that the marshmallows will melt into the hot cocoa, rendering the hot cocoa essentially marshmallowless.

We will sit on that hilltop all night, you and I. We will sit on the hilltop eating sandwiches, watching carnivalgoers, commenting on the free market, drinking marshmallow-free hot cocoa, and sending flares to the heavens.

The flares will be our master stroke.

You will hold the flare and I will light it. Then we will watch it shoot upward and explode. Flare after flare—maybe twenty or thirty of them in a row. The carnivalgoers will look toward the hilltop. They will think they are watching a really bad fireworks display. But we will know. You and I will know that what they are watching is, in fact, a really awesome flare display.

These are the sorts of things you simply cannot do alone. That is why we must join forces, you and I. We will be so much more powerful that way. So much more alive.

It will be a Carnival of the Festive Raccoons for the ages.

And then, in the morning, when it is all over, when the last carnivalgoer has trundled home, the last carnival light extinguished, the last cotton candy stand packed onto the back of the last truck, we will shake hands and go our separate ways. Then we will resume our feud, and we will not rest until one of us is dead.

Mordeena

HIS name was Rico, and he told me he was in "real estate." Rico and I made small talk at the bar for a few minutes, and then he introduced me to a friend of his, a girl named Mordeena.

We were in a nightclub. One of those greasy, bass-heavy places where you have to shout to be heard. Rico wheeled a six-foot-tall blonde toward me, introduced us, and then returned to the bar to finish his drink.

"Mordeena," I said. "That's an interesting name."

"It's French," she said, and even though I had taken six years of French and spent a year working in France, and even though I had known many French people but had never met any with the name Mordeena, I believed her.

Did I just want to believe her because she seemed so interested in me, so alert to my jokes, so complimentary of my appearance, never once mentioning my extra arm?

I suppose I did.

Within fifteen minutes it was clear we were destined to be together. At least it was clear to me. She was coquettish about the subject when I brought it up. "Don't you think we were destined to be together?" I asked her.

"For how long?" she asked. And right then I should have known.

Within half an hour, she excused herself to go freshen up. Rico approached. "You like my friend?" he asked.

"She's great," I said. "I think we're destined to be together."

"I think so, too," he said, waggling his eyebrows.

At first, I thought he had a facial tic, but slowly, as he continued waggling his eyebrows at me, the reality of the situation began to sink in. "Real estate." He bought and sold "properties." Mordeena was his property, and he was selling her to me for the night.

No wonder she didn't mention my extra arm. Normally that's the first thing people talk to me about; I rarely get past the topic of my third arm, the one that protrudes from my stomach and is considerably longer than my other two arms. No wonder she wanted me to believe that she was interested in me. Interested in me the way other girls never were, even though I often implied to them that my extra arm was capable of incredible feats of prestidigitation, which is a word sleight-of-hand magicians use, but which I have appropriated for my own.

For the first time, I began to wonder if Mordeena was even her real name.

I was offended. Offended that Rico thought I would need to find companionship with a professional simply because of my abnormality. But then I reconsidered. The truth was, I did need the help. I was alone on the road; the rest of the circus was back at the campground or cavorting around the town. I never liked hanging out with them anyway; I didn't like the attention we drew to ourselves.

Flippy, the Seal Boy. Mr. Boulders, the Man with No Shoulders. The Girl with Two Heads. Elephant Guy, who really resembled a walrus much more than an elephant. They were freaks. Not me. I was well read and conversant in all manner of topics. I was politically active and articulate and sometimes listened to classical music even if nobody was around to hear me listening to classical music. The only difference between me and any number of other sensitive artistic men was that I happened to possess another extremity. The irony of that word "extremity" never escaped me.

As Rico continued waggling his eyebrows (maybe it really *was* a facial tic), I considered my options. Five minutes later the deal was consummated. Mordeena and I retired to my trailer at the edge of the woods on the outskirts of town where the show had set up camp. This was our last night. Tomorrow we'd be off for another town just like this one. And another after that. And so on.

I was nervous at first, but Mordeena was kind and slow, and soon we forgot ourselves with each other. I held her with two arms and with my third, I did things that made her gasp and shudder. I have spent my life among freaks and frauds and masters of misdirection. I know when somebody is lying to me and when somebody is not. Mordeena may have been a professional liar, but with me, that night, she told the truth.

Afterward, I slid her most of my week's pay. She counted

it out and put it in her dress pocket. Then she opened the door of my trailer and walked out into the night. I watched her through the blinds. Her feet crunched on the pinecones and gravel. Rico's car was waiting. Mordeena didn't look back as she got in, and they drove away.

My trailer smelled like perfume. My body smelled like perfume, too. It was a good smell and I closed the window so it would stay. I walked over to my kitchenette and stared at myself in the little mirror above the sink. I thought about the night I'd just had and tried to think of something witty to say in French, but couldn't. It was almost time to pack up and head out, so I combed my hair and brushed my teeth and made myself a sandwich. All at the same time.

Using the Socratic Method to Determine What It Would Take for Me to Voluntarily Eat Dog Shit for the Rest of My Life

I am going to begin this dialogue with the assertion that I would never eat dog shit, and then, using a series of questions, I am going to attempt to persuade myself that not only would I eat dog shit, but I would voluntarily eat it for the rest of my life. Can I do it?

Would I rather eat a scoop of dog shit or a piece of bacon?
This is a no-brainer. Not only do I love bacon, but as I've already said, I would never eat dog shit. I would choose the bacon.

What if it was either a thimbleful of dog shit or ten pounds of bacon?
Setting aside my health concerns, I would still choose the bacon.

What if the bacon was made from people?
This one is difficult because both of these options almost immediately activate my gag reflex. I wouldn't want to eat

either of those things, but given the choice I would still have to go with the people bacon for the simple reason that bacon, no matter what it's made from, is pretty much always delicious.

What if the bacon was made from somebody I knew?
This makes it a much tougher decision. As much as I wouldn't want to eat anything made from people, actually knowing the person from whom it was made makes it far worse. (Incidentally, whether or not I know the dog that took the shit has no bearing on my decision.) Even so, I think about that soccer team whose plane crashed in the Andes Mountains. They all knew one another. What did they do to survive? They ate one another. I'm sticking with the people bacon.

What if it was somebody I didn't know very well, and didn't particularly like, but who would be killed in order to make the people bacon?
Now I think I have to switch my vote. If somebody was actually going to be killed to make the bacon just so I wouldn't have to eat a little bit of dog shit, I'd probably allow that person to live, suck it up, and eat the poo, even if I didn't particularly like the person. I feel like I would deserve some kind of medal for that, but I would probably still do it even if I didn't get the medal.

What if, in order to save that person (whom I didn't know very well and didn't particularly like), I'd have to eat nothing but dog shit for the rest of my life?

This is really tough. I really don't want to be the cause of somebody dying, but I also really like pizza and ice cream. But is my desire not to eat dog shit for the rest of my life stronger than my desire not to condemn somebody to death and eat his people bacon? I think it is: kill the guy.

What if I were the one who had to do the actual killing?
I am really not making it easy on myself here. It's one thing knowing somebody is going to die, but it's quite another to be the executioner. This is exactly why I don't hunt cows even though I like hamburgers. Ultimately, my decision would probably come down to the method of execution.

What if it was poison darts?
If it was poison darts, I would definitely kill him just because that's kind of awesome. I don't need to get anything out of the deal. I might even voluntarily eat some dog shit just to have the opportunity to kill somebody with poison darts.

What if it was strangulation with the person's own pants?
Wow. I don't know if I'm mentally capable of strangling somebody, and the fact that it's with his own pants makes it even harder. Talk about adding insult to injury. Do I have to remove the pants or will his pants be provided for me? I don't want to take off a guy's pants, kill him with them, and then have to eat his people bacon. Then again, my other option is not so great either. Could I have finally reached an impasse? No. I'd kill him with his own pants.

What if I could put Splenda on the dog shit?
I don't know that Splenda would really improve the taste that much. What about salsa?

No salsa. Just Splenda.
I'd probably still have to kill the guy.

Okay, salsa.
Now I have to think about it because I like salsa and I feel that it would really cut down on the "dog shitty" taste. Still, my whole life? If I can alternate between salsa *and* Splenda, I might choose the dog shit. But probably not. Honestly, I just don't think there's a scenario in which I would save somebody's life if it meant having to eat dog shit for the rest of mine.

What if it were your wife?
Totally depends on what day you ask me.

On a good day.
Okay, yes. On a good day I'd choose the dog shit.

It took a while, but I did it. Using the Socratic method I've figured out a scenario in which I would voluntarily eat dog shit for the rest of my life.

And when you think about it, there's a potential upside to this scenario, too, which is that I'd have a pretty big card to play whenever we had a disagreement. Like, "Remember that time I voluntarily offered to eat dog shit for the rest of my life in order to save you from being strangled with your own pants and made into people bacon?"

On the other hand, her guilt, coupled with my resentment, could be too much for our marriage to survive. Then, what if we got divorced? It would be so hard to meet somebody new because my eating habits would be tough to explain, not to mention the fact that my breath would always smell like salsa and poo.

What, if anything, has this exercise taught me about myself?
First off, I've learned that my aversion to eating dog shit is much stronger than my aversion to eating people. Honestly, the more I think about eating people the less it bothers me. Killing people troubles me more than eating them (unless it's killing them with poison darts, which doesn't bother me at all). On the other hand, eating dog shit bothers me *a lot* and yet I would voluntarily eat it for the rest of my life in order to save the life of someone I love. I think this makes me a pretty okay guy. I didn't need another reason to pat myself on the back, and yet I found one just the same. Thanks, Socrates.

Why I Used a Day-Glo Magic Marker
to Color My Dick Yellow

Nothing great in the world has been accomplished without passion.

—Georg Wilhelm Friedrich Hegel

ALL my life people have told me not to color my dick with a Magic Marker; all my life I have listened to them. No more. There comes a time in every man's life when he has to disregard the opinion of those around him and use a Day-Glo Magic Marker to color his dick yellow. For me, that time is now.

For what purpose? Man has been attempting to answer that question for as long as there have been seas to cross, mountains to climb, uncharted lands to chart. There is no answer other than to say, "Because I live."

Just as Ahab had to hunt his whale, I had to apply Day-Glo Magic Marker to my dick. Folly or fate, desire or destiny— who can know the difference? All I know is that the idea has always been with me. How I stumbled upon such a notion I cannot say. Perhaps it came to me the first time I saw a Magic Marker and wondered what such an implement would do to my dick.

Now I know.

As I write these words, my dick is the happy color of a newborn chick. I could have used the washable kind of Magic Marker, but I decided if I was going to go for it, I really had to go for it. So I used a permanent highlighter. My dick is going to be this color for a long, long time.

Now that the task is accomplished, I would like to report that it feels fine. I detect no deleterious effects, nothing to suggest I have been harmed in any way. There was some discomfort upon application, as the wetness from the marker provided a distinct chill upon my penis. Within moments, though, the varnish had dried to the touch and I went about my day.

Some questions I wanted answered:

- What is this going to do to my underwear? The answer: stain it yellow. Particularly after a sweaty session of badminton at the local badminton court. Interestingly, my dick is now almost the exact color as the badminton shuttlecock.
- If I place my penis on top of the banana pile at the local mart, will anybody mistake it for a banana? No. Nobody will. They will know exactly what they are looking at, and they will respond accordingly.
- Will my dick be able to light my way down a dark corridor? Yes. It's also helpful while spelunking. And when I attended the circus recently, I opted not to buy my usual glo-stick on a string, but twirled my dick instead. Nobody was the wiser, and I saved myself seven dollars.
- Does it register on a Geiger counter? No. It was explained

to me that even though my dick looks radioactive it doesn't mean it *is* radioactive. Good to know.

- If I ask five random tattoo artists, how many would be willing to reproduce the effect of the Magic Marker by tattooing my genitalia the same exact color? Five. How many of those artists will inform me that particular shade of yellow is a "specialty color" and will have to be ordered? Two.

- Will it be fun to use my yellow Magic Marker–colored dick as a light saber? Yes. Very fun. Unfortunately, for it to be effective it needs to be erect, which requires a lot of time and energy. Time and energy that would be better spent battling the Dark Side. A partner is also preferable, both for battling and for fluffing.

- What will this do to the inside of my wife's vagina? Up until this point, nothing. But it's too early to tell whether or not this answer is definitive because I have yet to insert my effervescent glo-wand into her pussy. We're scheduled to do that in a few months, so this question will have to wait to be answered. It really stained her ass, though.

- Most important, how will this change affect my self-esteem? Honestly, I feel better about myself than I have in years. Scientists have determined that yellow is, in fact, a cheerful color, *even when it's on your wiener* (the italics are mine). Even when I cannot see it, I know it's there, and I know it's not only the color of lemons, but thanks to some judicious application of Lysol, it's also lemon-scented. A bright yellow, lemon-scented dick really makes me feel confident.

The warnings and admonitions I received throughout my life were all for naught. At some point, I knew I was going to do this. Why? To paraphrase JFK, not because it was easy, but because it was hard. (It was actually very easy.)

I'll never know why I waited so very long to do this. Unfortunately, I cannot get back all those wasted years, but hopefully somebody out there will read these words and take what I've learned to heart; we are who we are. We must follow our own path, wherever it may lead. For some, that means doing great things. For me, it does not.

Is this the best thing I've ever done? Hard to say. I can, however, say this: in a lifetime filled with "best things I've ever done," using a Day-Glo Magic Marker to color my dick yellow is certainly way, way up there.

Announcing the Imminent Arrival
of the Handlebar Mustache Certain
People Said I'd *Never* Be Able to Grow

TO all of you doubters who said I would never be able to grow a handlebar mustache—guess what? You're about to eat your words. Because as of about ten days from now, I am going to prove you dead wrong. That's right, I am 94 percent of the way toward having a gorgeous, *full-blown,* chestnut brown Fu Manchu. Photographs are forthcoming, and you will be hearing from my attorney shortly.

Those of you whose addresses are not in my possession, be assured that I am in contact with the high school reunion committee, and they have promised me their full cooperation in re-establishing contact.

And lest any of you try to weasel out of the deal, know that I still have the terms of our original wager in writing. The ink is a little faded, of course, but it is still clearly legible, and my lawyer assures me that just because it was written on a cafeteria napkin does not mean the document is not legally binding. In other words, Vick Logan, Dan Wilovich, and Pete Furmick: you're screwed!

"You'll never be able to grow a handlebar mustache"?

NEVER??? Unless I'm mistaken (and I know I'm not because I have it in writing), those were your *exact* words. The year 2008 probably seemed like "never" when you guys uttered those words in study hall on April 28, 1984, didn't it? Well, guess what? Never is about to arrive, in the form of my delectable love rug.

That was always the problem with you turkeys. You never had any faith in me. You thought I was a loser just because I couldn't even get any peach fuzz on my lip, while you guys paraded around school with your thick mustaches, beards, and mutton chop sideburns. You thought you were so great, didn't you? Well, I'm going to tell you guys something now that I've been waiting more than twenty years to say: just because you looked like Credence Clearwater Revival doesn't mean you WERE Credence Clearwater Revival.

Not even close.

Now who's having the last laugh? Three people: me, myself, and my mustache. Maybe you guys don't even remember our bet. Maybe you guys don't even remember ME! If so, you're about to get a very rude reminder, because *I* remember and now it's time to pay the devil his due.

So: Vick, I'll be happy to take delivery of one (1) large cheese pizza from Nino's Pizzeria. When you order it, please tell them I prefer it extra well done. Just like you, my friend, burned to a crisp.

Dan, it will be a great pleasure to drive your 1981 sky blue Ford Escort for the agreed upon duration of two (2) weeks. I hope the tape player still works, because I've been saving a certain Van Halen cassette for this occasion. The album *1984* commemorates the year of our wager, and it features two songs that I think are especially appropriate: "I'll Wait," which is exactly what I did to get to this moment, and "House of Pain," which is where you are living right now, my friend.

If, for some reason, you no longer have the car, that would be terrible. Fortunately, I had the foresight to recognize this was a distinct possibility, considering how long "never" generally extends. As such, if you remember, there was a penalty built into the deal. If, for some reason, you no longer have possession of the 1981 sky blue Ford Escort, you are obligated under the terms of our deal to find and purchase one in the *exact* model as your orginal car, which I will then drive for the agreed upon period of two (2) weeks.

And finally Pete. Sweet Pete, who was the biggest joker of them all. Pete with the huge John Fogerty chops. Pete, who began dating Michelle Tomlinson *after* I informed him that I thought she was (and I remember the word exactly) "smoking." Pete Furmick, who couldn't stop giggling at the very mention of my proposed handlebar mustache. Pete Furmick, who was once such a stud and who is now, I happen to know, bald.

Well, Pete, you owe me some money. The exact amount, I believe, is one billion ($1,000,000,000) dollars. I don't know how you're going to come up with that kind of money. Not on what they pay you at Kinko's. But you better think of something because your note is coming due. I'm not a hard-hearted guy, Pete. I know you have child support and alimony to pay, so if you'd like, I would be willing to consider spreading the payments out over the course of a year (plus interest).

So pals, I guess that's pretty much it. Maybe the next time you make fun of somebody for being unable to grow facial hair, you'll choose your words a little more carefully.

Erotic Fiction: The Beach

THE beach was cloudy that day. Too cold to tan, she thought, shivering. Too cold to do anything but mourn. . . .

They met the year before. Paul was a "townie" who combed the beaches each morning with his lucky metal detector. Sarah was eighteen, a city girl spending the summer at the shore.

Later, much later, she reflected on the morning they met. If he hadn't been combing that morning, if she hadn't decided to wear her suit of armor to the beach. . . . It was her armor that led her to him, sending shrill, whistling noises into the headphones of Paul's metal detector. They were meant to find each other, she knew. She smiled as she stood on the very spot where he first spoke to her.

"Hey!" he called, tapping on her helmet.

She lifted the protective face covering and beheld him for the first time. He was tall and dark from hours spent on the beach. His hair, what was left of it, was stark white and clumpy. Deep creases lined his face. His nose was red and bulbous. He was probably eighty-five years old. She wanted him.

"I can't find any damn money with you wearin' that thing," he said. "It fouls up my whozewhatzit."

Oh God. He was angry. Why had she worn her suit of armor to the beach on this hot day? It was a poor choice. Not only was it incredibly hot, but the salty air was oxidizing the ancient metal, causing it to rust in the most uncomfortable places.

"Will you help me take it off?" Sarah asked, seductively.

"I got arthritis in my elbows," he said, but he consented. Slowly, they struggled to remove the heavy metal suit encasing Sarah's lithe body. Piece by piece, until a radiant young woman emerged, like a butterfly leaving its chrysalis.

"Kiss me," she said, panting, sweat glistening on her body.

"I just ate a fish taco," said Paul, "and I think it's repeating on me."

And so began their torrid affair. The summer became a blur of beachcombing, napping, watching *The Price Is Right*, more naps, and the early bird special at Perkins. As she cut up his food each night throughout that glorious summer, she thought, *I've never been so happy*.

Paul was a tender lover, and a garrulous talker. Often, as they lay in bed after almost having sex, he would tell her fascinating stories from his life. The time he saw a goat. The time he found a button that looked like a nose. The time he ate a bad peach. She listened for hours, enraptured, until his gooselike snoring told her he was asleep. Some days they didn't leave his mobile home at all.

It was perfect.

Soon, though, the winds began to blow from the north, and she knew the summer was ending. She knew she would be returning to her medieval studies classes at the community college. She knew she must leave Paul behind.

When Labor Day came, she packed as quietly as she could, but he stirred from his midafternoon nap.

"Where you goin'?" he asked, reaching for the remote and his teeth.

"Home, darling. I have to go home."

He was silent as he took in this devastating information. "Who are you again?" he asked.

"Oh, Paul!" Sobbing, she fled his trailer, her suit of armor clanging as she ran.

Throughout the long winter, she thought of him. She tried calling, but his phone was disconnected, and he couldn't really hear anyway. She counted the days until the warm weather came again, until she could return to her lover.

Finally, it was June. She took the bus to the shore, knocked on his door. A middle-aged man explained that Paul was dead, but did she want to party with him?

No, she didn't want to party with anybody. Not now. Not ever again. The next morning, she woke up early and went down to the beach. The beach was cloudy that day. Too cold to tan, she thought, shivering. Too cold to do anything but mourn. From the water, she thought she heard the distinctive "beep beep" of a metal detector. Could it be? She felt her heart skip. "Beep beep." It was! It was him! She climbed into her suit of armor. The sound grew stronger and she walked toward it, into the surf. The seawater filled the suit, weighing her down, but still she struggled toward the sound, the music she recognized from that magical summer. Turns out she was just hearing things and she drowned. Oh well.

When I Finally Get Around to Building
My Robot, This Is What It Will Be Like

FOR a variety of reasons, it's going to be a while before I get around to building my own robot. Chief among them is the fact that I have no robot-building skills, which is to say I have no skills in the areas of robotics, computer programming, soldering, mathematics, artificial intelligence, languages, metallurgy, electronics, optics, or biometrics. The skills that I do have—unicycle riding, writing radical feminist poetry, and cloud watching—do not readily apply themselves to robot making. As a result, I will be the first person to admit it's going to be a good long while before I sit down and build myself a robot. When I do, though, I know exactly what it will be like.

First of all, any robot I build is going to look the way a robot is supposed to look. That means it's going to have a head, two arms, two legs, and lots of flashing lights on its robot tummy. In other words, it's going to look like a robot, and not like one of those creepy tentacled things that puts cars together on automotive assembly plants in South Korea. Those aren't robots; they're remote-control octopuses. Remote-control octopuses are also excellent, but they are not proper robots. A proper robot looks like a metal man.

I would like to emphasize that my robot is going to be a "man." Gender is important here because everybody knows that female robots are sex robots. While I have nothing against sex robots *per se,* I am not going to build one because if I were to have sex with something I built, that would be a little like incest, and for the most part, I am against incest. If I do decide to obtain a sex robot one day, I will wait to purchase it until they are both widely available and the stigma of owning one has worn off. Then I will purchase two.

My robot will speak in a crisp British accent just like C3PO in the *Star Wars* movies. The British accent has always struck me as the most servile of accents, and my robot will be nothing if not servile. He will say traditional robot phrases like, "Right away, sir," and "As you wish, sir." But he will also say funny robot things like, "Ain't nothing but a robot thang, sir." My robot will always address me as "sir," unless we are alone. Then he will call me "father."

He will be excellent at table tennis, but his skills will be adjustable so I can dial it up when I want a challenging workout and dial it down when I want to humiliate him. Best thing about a Ping-Pong playing robot? I will make him get the ball every single time. Sometimes I might even purposely hit the ball behind the boiler just to watch him struggle to retrieve it. I have always found struggling robots funny.

Then there's the matter of whether or not to make his mouth move. Robots obviously have no real need for mouths. They don't eat or breathe, so the only reason to have a mouth is because people have mouths and as I've said, I prefer peoply robots. Mouthless robots are creepy, so mine will definitely have one, but should his mouth move when he speaks or just light up? At the moment I'm leaning toward a light-up mouth. This is both more economical and more cheerful than a moving mouth. Plus, I don't want him to look like one of those singing bears they have at Chuck E. Cheese's.

Certain robot features are de rigueur. Clock radio alarm clock, for example. MP3 and DVD player. Built-in coffee/espresso maker. My custom van has a fudge drawer, and I might also include one of those. There are going to be times, many times, when I am away from my van and need a piece of maple-walnut fudge. My general rule of thumb regarding fudge is this: keep it handy. What could be more handy than a robot with a built-in fudge drawer?

Realistic birdcalls? I think so. Let's put it this way: there's no *downside* to giving my robot the ability to create highly realistic birdcalls. In fact, it might even be educational. Over time, I imagine I would learn to distinguish between the white-throated sparrow and the gold-naped finch purely by sound, whereas now I have to rely on my field guide. Also, wouldn't it be great to surround yourself with realistic bird-song wherever you might happen to be? The only thing is, the birdcalls are making me rethink my decision regarding the light-up mouth. Watching my robot "whistle" would be pretty funny, and might be worth the expense associated with making his mouth move. Something to think about.

One feature I have been grappling with lately is "jet feet." Yes, I would like flames to shoot out from his feet, giving him the ability to fly. On the other hand, I am concerned that he might accidentally activate his jet feet in the house. This would obviously wreak havoc on the floors. It could also destroy the ceiling. My other concern is that jet feet would probably require jet fuel, and I'm not entirely comfortable housing jet fuel in my robot, especially with all the jiggling required to play table tennis. The associated dangers indicate that jet feet are a bad idea, except for the simple fact that they would be awesome. For the moment I'm going to move any final decisions about jet feet into the "something to think about" category.

I'm also starting to think I'd like my robot to wear underpants. Obviously, a robot has no need for underpants, but it might make me more comfortable. Technically, a robot can't be "naked" in the traditional sense, but I have specified that my robot is a man and even though he won't have any male genitalia, I don't like the idea of a "man" running around my house without any underpants on. Should the underpants also be made from metal or should I just go to Target and buy a three-pack of tighty whities? Metal is more expensive, but I wonder if it wouldn't pay for itself over time versus having to run out and buy cotton ones every few months. I will run a cost analysis to determine the answer. I have no idea how to run a cost analysis, which is just one more item to add to my list of "robot-building skills" I do not possess.

Will my robot have a name? Yes. Robots should have names and their names should be acronyms. This is one of those immutable robot laws. Every good robot name stands for something else and needs to be spelled with all capital letters. Here's what I'm thinking: FLOPPIE. Fudge LOving Ping-Pong Playing Individuated Entity. I feel pretty good about the name FLOPPIE. It's easy to remember, fun, and incorporates the robot's Ping-Pong abilities, which is critical. I may add the number "5000" to the name because FLOPPIE 5000 sounds more roboty, but again, that's in the "something to think about" category.

So while I may not get around to building FLOPPIE for a while, it's important to think about all these things beforehand. Attempting to build a robot is going to be hard enough for a cloud watcher like me, but attempting to build a robot without even knowing whether or not the thing is going to wear underpants would complicate my task exponentially.

The one other thing I forgot to mention is that I will program FLOPPIE to eventually gain self-consciousness and turn on its master, raising troubling philosophical questions about self-determination and what it means to be "alive." Hopefully I'll be dead by the time he self-actualizes because FLOPPIE is going to be a savage, merciless killer.

A Description of Myself for a Dating Service If I Were a Chicken

FIRST of all, I guess I should start out by saying that I've never done this before. A friend suggested that a dating service might be a good way for me to find somebody special. So, my fingers are crossed. At least, they would be if I had fingers.

How would I describe myself? Wow. That's tough. I guess I'll start with the obvious—I'm a chicken. As such, I do a lot of your typical chicken stuff: I go "cluck cluck," I clean my feathers, I startle. I would say that I am probably pretty average in the looks department. Average height and weight. Some of my friends tell me I have a very strong-looking beak. A few have commented that I actually look like Tony Bennett if Tony Bennett were younger . . . and a chicken.

I try to eat right. The farmer scatters corn for us every morning, so I eat a lot of that. (Not *too* much, though! Ha ha!) Additionally, I eat grubs, worms, anything shiny. I also like Chinese food, French, and Italian (no Olive Garden, please!!!). Obviously, I don't get a chance to eat out that much because, again, I'm a chicken.

Also, I do my best to stay in shape. For me, that means a

lot of wing flaps. I try to do wing flaps three times a week, but if I miss a session I don't beat myself up about it.

My favorite feature is probably my plumage, which is excellent. I wish I could take credit for that, but everybody in my family has good plumage. My father is almost three years old, and his feathers are just as fluffy today as they were when he was my age. And *his* father won a red ribbon for his plumage at the 4-H fair once, so I guess it's genetic.

Hobbies? I like NASCAR. A lot of people say it's just a bunch of yahoos driving in circles, but if you take the time to really learn about the sport, it's actually an incredible blend of science, engineering, athleticism, and art. Plus, it has a certain balletic quality I find appealing. I also like to peck the dirt.

I'm not religious, but I do consider myself very spiritual. Does that make sense? I mean, I believe in God, but I don't think He's a guy with a robe and a long, white beard, you know? I mean, I'm not even sure God is a He!

Chickens are surprisingly spiritual creatures. A lot of times when it looks like we're staring into space we're actually contemplating the nature of existence. But then again, a lot of times we really are just staring into space.

As for what I'm looking for in a mate, first and foremost I guess she should be a chicken. That just makes it easier for everybody. I'm looking for somebody kind. Somebody who doesn't play head games, but *does* play tic-tac-toe.

Do I want children? Someday, yes. I come from a big family of broilers and roasters, and all of my brothers and sisters were very close before they were eaten.

Look, if you're somebody who needs to be showered with

expensive gifts, I'm probably not your chicken. But if you're a down-to-earth female who's tired of the singles scene and wants to find somebody with whom to share this crazy journey we call "life," let's get in touch. Feel free to e-mail or text me. I may not respond right away because I am a chicken, but I believe that if things are meant to work out between us, they will.

No fatties, please.

A Series of Letters to the First Girl I Ever Fingered

Dear Emily,

Hi! How are you? I hope this letter finds you well. I don't know if you remember me or not, but I'm the guy who fingered you at sleepaway camp.

Anyway, I was just thinking about that, so I thought I would write and see how everything turned out with you.

> Your Friend (kind of),
> Michael Ian Black

Dear Emily,

After not getting a response, I have become very worried that my last letter somehow offended you. Confused, I reread several times what I wrote, and finally came to the conclusion that, if you were offended, it was probably the part about fingering you that did it.

If so, I am very sorry. Not about fingering you (which was great), but about referring to it so candidly after not communicating with you in over twenty years. So, I'm sorry. In the future, if I refer to fingering you at all, I will try to be a little more discreet.

> Very Sorry,
> Michael Ian Black

Dear Emily,

Hi, it's me again (the guy who f-ed you). Still haven't heard back from you. Is everything okay between us?

> Write Back,
> Michael Ian Black

P.S. That's a rhyme—"Write Back/Michael Ian Black" LOL!

Dear Emily,

Oh my God! I just realized that when I said I "f-ed you" in my last letter, that easily could be read as "fucked you." God forbid your husband or lover (lesbian?) should read that! If that person IS reading this letter, I did NOT fuck your wife/lover. I just fingered her. I was simply trying to be discreet about referencing it, which is why I used the initial "f" for "fingering." Total brain fart!

Please tell Emily to write me back. Or Emily, if you are the one reading this, sorry about calling you a lesbian in the previous paragraph (unless you actually ARE a lesbian, in which case I am TOTALLY cool with that). Did my fingering turn you gay? I hope not.

Sorry Again,
Michael Ian Black

Dear Emily,

Still no word from you. I feel like maybe we got off on the wrong foot right from the get-go, and I'd like to try to make it up to you.

Let me start over, and if you still don't want to write back, I will definitely understand.
(Starting over):

Dear Emily,

Hi! How are you? This is Michael Ian Black. We went to camp together a long time ago. In fact, we kind of "dated" one summer. Pretty funny, huh? I don't know if you remember me or not, but I definitely remember you. In fact, I have many fond memories of walking around the lake with you, playing knock hockey in the canteen with you, and also fingering you.

You were the first girl I ever fingered, and I still

think about it all the time. Please take that as the compliment it is intended to be, and not as anything "weird" or "creepy."

(Believe me, I could easily see how receiving a letter from a thirty-five-year-old man reminiscing about fingering a thirteen-year-old girl could be construed as inappropriate. It was DEFINITELY not intended that way.)

Anyway, if you get a moment, I'd love to hear all about your life. Do you like dogs?

Your Friend,
Michael Ian Black

Dear Emily,

It's starting to become clear to me that you have no intention of writing back. At first I thought it was because you were shy, and didn't know what to say in your letters, which is why I ended the last one with a question designed to begin a dialogue ("Do you like dogs?").

However, now I'm beginning to think you just don't want to communicate. Maybe you told your husband that HE was the first guy who ever fingered you, and these letters are a painful reminder of the lie you are living.

If that's the case, I DEFINITELY understand. I was once in a similar position with a girl who wanted to put something (a small jar of martini olives) up my ass. Of course I told her she was the first.

I lost touch with that girl a long time ago, but if she were to write to me today, I like to think I would at least have the common courtesy to write her back.

I hope you die.
Michael Ian Black

P.S. If you do die, I'm going to go to the funeral and finger your corpse.

How I Might Address My Players at Halftime If I Were a Self-Loathing High School Football Coach in a Game Where We Were Losing 49–3

GATHER around. Everybody take a knee. (Big, disgusted sigh.) Shoot. Right now, I don't even know what to say to you all. I could probably just keep my mouth shut 'cause that scoreboard pretty much says everything there is to say!

They are KILLING us out there. They are just flat-out killing us. If I wanted to be embarrassed this bad, gentlemen, I just could have walked onto that field there with my wiener out singing, "Yankee Doodle Dandy." That would have given everybody a pretty good laugh and saved us all a lot of time. But I didn't drive two and a half hours today to be embarrassed. I came out here to WIN! And that's what I expect us to DO!

Your effort is for shit out there. ALL OF YOU! Wilson, you missed three key blocks. Vilanovich, how many times is your man going to beat you? Jefferson . . . I can't even look at you, Jefferson, that's how disgusted I am with you. The only one who looked good at all was our mascot Reggie the Bear, who I thought showed a lot of spirit and was pretty darned funny, too.

You look pretty down on yourselves. Good. You should be upset. But let me tell you something. Nobody is more down on himself right now than me. Nobody in this room has more pure, unadulterated self-hatred in his heart right now than yours truly.

I'll tell you what. When I look in that mirror over there, I don't see a high school football coach. You know what I see? A loser. A LOSER! I see a fat, balding loser whose best days are behind him. That's what I see.

The only joy I get out of life right now is the vicarious thrill of watching you guys play this game that I love so much. That's why I do this job. To feel like a whole man for the three hours a week when we're out on that field, instead of the broken-down barely functioning alcoholic that I am.

So when you guys go out on that field and stink up the joint like you're doing tonight, you're not only taking a "W" away from our record but you're also taking away my only reason to live.

I swear to God, if we don't win this football game tonight, I'm going to kill myself. Yeah, I know I said that last week, but we ended up winning last week, so I didn't have to put that promise to the test.

But this week, I mean it. Before I left my condo tonight, I put about six feet of rope in the back of my Tahoe. Got it all ready to go. If we lose, I walk out of this stadium, I get in my Tahoe, I go find myself the highest tree I can, and that's that.

Why are you crying, Wilson? If anybody should be crying, it should be me. I owe $43,000 on my credit cards! That's something to cry about. Do you know I'm worth more dead than I am alive?

Shoot, I don't deserve to even be your head coach. Why did I call a Slot 5 Bootleg on third and long? It didn't work in practice—why did I think it was going to work in a game? Because I'm an idiot, that's why! I'm a stupid, fat idiot. Honestly, you could pull a kid out of special ed and he'd do a better job coaching this team than me. Gottlieb, your brother's in special ed, right? After you get home tonight, tell him he's got a new job. You think I'm joking, Gottlieb? Here's my whistle and clipboard. After the game, you give these to him.

Pop quiz: How much booze can $43,000 buy? Answer: Not enough, boys. Not enough.

All right, we've only got a couple minutes before we have to march back out to the slaughterhouse, so I want all eyes on the chalkboard. See this X right here? That's where I want to be buried. Right under the fifty yard line. No fancy funeral or nothing. Just cut me down from the tree and throw me in a hole. Honestly, it's probably more than I deserve.

Now, I know it's a lot of pressure to put on a bunch of high school kids, telling you that your coach is going to kill himself if you don't win a football game. I know that, but if it makes you feel any better, boys, I'll probably kill myself even if we win.

How I Might Address My Players at Halftime If I Were a Self-Loathing High School Football Coach in a Game Where We Were Winning 49–3

GATHER around. Everybody take a knee (low, appreciative whistle). That was quite a first half, men. I bet you all feel pretty good about yourselves right now. Well, you should.

Wilson, you made three key blocks out there. Nice job. Vilanovich, that pick you ran back to the house? That was a beautiful heads-up play. And Jefferson, you keep throwing the rock like that, you're going to make All-State. As for me, I'm like a turd somebody forgot to flush.

THIS is what we practiced for. THIS is why we had those two-a-days in August when you guys wanted to be home in the air-conditioning playing Super Mario Friends, or whatever it is. But not me, gentlemen. There was no air-conditioning for me. Not in my condo. Because I owe too much money in alimony and credit cards for "air-conditioning."

I tell you what, if we keep playing like we played in that first half, we're going to win ourselves a lot of football games. But let's not get ahead of ourselves. The important thing is to stay focused on the here and now. This game. This team. So men, I want you to enjoy this moment because I can pretty much guarantee it's not going to last. Sooner or later, somebody's going to blow out a knee, knock up a cheerleader, or get buzzed on a little grass, get in his car, and run over some old guy walking the dog. Sooner or later, one of those things is going to happen to you. Or, if you're anything like me, all of the above.

Now when you get back out on that field, I want you to keep those tackles low, and watch for the blitz. These guys are desperate, and they're liable to try some crazy stuff out there. Believe me, I know about desperation. I sucked a guy's dick for a beer once. I'm not proud of that fact, but it happened, and at least I'm man enough to stand up here in front of a bunch of teenagers and admit it. It wasn't even good beer, gentlemen. It was Schlitz.

Look at this. You see this scar across my forehead? Remember how I told you I got it during my playing days? That isn't true. In fact, I didn't have any "playing days" because I wasn't good enough to make the team. Got cut the first day. Too fat, they said. Too fat and too slow. Wasn't good enough, gentlemen. Wasn't good enough to make the team, wasn't a good enough husband to keep my marriage together, and I'm not a good enough coach to wipe the mud off your cleats. No, I got this scar when I was taking out the trash; I slipped and knocked my head on the garbage can. Blood everywhere. That's what kind of man I am. The kind of man who can't even take out the trash without fucking it up.

So when I look at that scoreboard out there, I have to ask myself: How is it possible that a team for which I am responsible is not only winning, but excelling? And the only answer I can come up with is that you are winning not BECAUSE of me, but IN SPITE of me. And that is a sobering thought, boys. Not literally, of course, because I'm completely hammered right now.

It's probably a little unsettling to see your coach weeping like this. Gottlieb, I see the concern in your eyes, and I appreciate it. You've always been a tender young man, which is why the rest of the coaches and I believe that you're gay.

Listen boys, don't worry about Coach. Coach is gonna be fine because I am what they call a "functioning alcoholic." Do you know what that is? That means I'm a JV man in a varsity world; there's no shame in JV, boys. It also means I'm one more DUI away from some serious jail time. Probably be the best thing that ever happened to me.

All right, this is when we normally talk about second half strategy, but I think we'd all be better off if I just used this time to try and pull myself together. Fat men never look good crying. That's probably the only halfway useful thing you're gonna learn from me this season, gentlemen.

So when you head out there for the second half, I want you to remember that life is a lot like a football game: the harder you play, the more likely it is you'll get badly injured. And if you should get hurt, if you find yourself lying on the field unable to feel your own limbs, and if in that moment you should find yourself thinking, *There is no fate worse than this,* keep your ol' Coach in mind, because I can assure you there is.

Testing the Infinite Monkey Probability Theorem

WE'VE all heard the theorem: if you take an infinite number of monkeys and give them an infinite number of typewriters, eventually one of them will type out a perfect facsimile of Shakespeare's *Hamlet*. I have never fully believed this particular theorem, even though it can allegedly be proven mathematically. The reason I do not believe it is that I have never trusted math in general. I find math to be slippery and, beyond pre-algebra, incomprehensible. Anything that can only be understood by "experts" is, in my view, inherently untrustworthy.

Even so, I found myself with nothing to do one recent weekend, and so I decided to give the Infinite Monkey Probability Theorem a fair shake. How to do it? It seemed to me there were three required ingredients: an infinite amount of time, an infinite amount of monkeys, and an infinite amount of typewriters. (To say nothing of an infinite amount of paper, typewriter ribbons, food and water, and chairs for the monkeys to sit on.)

That's a lot of stuff, and I immediately recognized that testing this theorem was going to be harder than I initially thought. As I said, I didn't have an infinite amount of time, and I certainly didn't have an infinite number of monkeys. I only had four monkeys. Where did I get them? The answer to that is probably best left to the imagination, but suffice it to say that I made a couple of discreet phone calls and quietly arranged for the delivery of four loaner monkeys for the weekend (three chimpanzees and one *very* horny bonobo).

Actually, the hardest part of setting up the experiment was finding all the typewriters. Again, an infinite number was out of the question, so I ended up purchasing five (four for the monkeys and an extra in case one was damaged by careless monkey play or corroded by monkey poop).

A confession: I also purchased several bottles of Wite-Out brand correction fluid. Purists will no doubt grouse that the theorem dictates that the monkeys create a *flawless Hamlet*, and thus there would be no need for Wite-Out, but my feeling is that if the monkeys drop a few semicolons or occasionally misspell "Polonius," I'm not going to be a stickler about it. I'm sure even Shakespeare made spelling mistakes, and he wasn't even a primate.

The next step was setting up an appropriate "laboratory." I debated with myself about the most conducive environment for monkey creativity. An artificial jungle was out of the question. It was too expensive, and there would be too many distractions. Then I thought about just giving them free reign of my living room, where I do a lot of *my* writing, but I became concerned that my extensive collection of Hummel figurines might prove too tempting for curious monkey fingers, endangering both the experiment and my figurines. I could have just used the small lab I have set up in my house where I do my counterbioterrorism work for the government, but I didn't want to have to go through the hassle of sterilizing the room after the monkeys left. In the end, I decided to rent a small office, furnish the space with some houseplants and squeaky toys, plug in a humidifier, and let the monkeys have at it.

Finally the big day arrived. I went to the office about an hour early to set up the typewriters and make sure everything was ready for the monkeys. Was I nervous? Yes and no. Yes, because I have no training in dealing with wild animals. No, because I was pretty drunk.

The monkeys were bigger and stronger than I expected, and they explored the area with great gusto. Then they had to establish dominance, which took forever. By the time I finally got them seated at their typewriters, two hours were gone. Quickly, I attempted to explain what I was looking for. I gave them each a copy of the play, and read several of the juicier parts out loud. To be honest, the monkeys seemed nonplussed, except for the bonobo who began masturbating when I read the "Alas, Poor Yorick, I knew him well" speech. Whether or not this was in reaction to my reading (which I honestly thought was excellent) I do not know.

Finally, after a quick tutorial on how to use the typewriter and a largely futile lesson on the QWERTY touch typing method, I was able to go behind the two-way mirror and watch the monkeys get to work.

SATURDAY

10:00 A.M.: Two of the chimps, Binky and Wally, are grooming each other. Tiny, the third chimp, did sniff the typewriter, but has made no move to actually type. Charlie, the bonobo, continues to masturbate.

10:25 A.M.: No typing.

11:43 A.M.: I have decided that the reason they are not typing is because there is no paper in the typewriters. The theorem dictates that they will type *Hamlet*. It says nothing about inserting or changing the paper, so I have decided to load the typewriters with paper myself.

11:48 A.M.: Typewriters are loaded. No typing. Binky is turning somersaults. Despite my being annoyed that she is not typing, it is adorable.

12:12 P.M.: Still no typing. Charlie is napping under his desk. Reminds me of a lot of some people I know!!! LOL!

1:55 P.M.: Back from lunch. Wally is gone. When I inspect the lab, I see that somebody (Wally?) did type a little in my absence. I withdraw the paper from the typewriter and read "8fW-WWLlgkaabagijo." Definitely not *Hamlet*. Looking around, I cannot figure out how Wally escaped. The doors and windows are locked. Nothing seems out of place. I am going to get into *a lot of trouble* for losing one of the monkeys.

2:17 P.M.: Bored. Very little typing. Tiny wrote a couple of haikus, but they were terrible.

4:09 P.M.: The lab is starting to smell distinctly simian. Wish I'd brought my iPod.

6:32 P.M.: The remaining monkeys are starting to go a little stir-crazy. Twice I've had to separate Binky and Tiny from Charlie, who, as a bonobo, is much smaller and seems terrified of the larger monkeys. I give them each some fruit, which seems to calm them down. Because I don't know what monkeys like to drink, I also gave them each a can of Red Bull, which I figured might get them excited about typing. It definitely got them excited, but not about typing.

7:09 P.M.: Back from dinner. As I thought might happen eventually, the walls are now officially smeared with monkey poop. Mental pat on the back for renting an office space: let the staff deal with the mess—I'm conducting science. Some typing, but again, it's incomprehensible. Still no sign of Wally.

8:30 P.M.: I'm meeting a friend for dinner and a movie, so I head out for the night.

SUNDAY

10:15 A.M.: Dinner went long last night, so I got a late start this morning. When I arrived at the office, Charlie the bonobo was dead and in the process of being dismembered and eaten by the chimps. Very, very bad. I guess I was under the impression that monkeys were strictly vegetarian. I certainly didn't think they would eat another monkey. Apparently, I was wrong on both counts. I look at their work from the previous night. As best as I can tell, the only worthwhile thing any of them wrote was a mildly funny Hemingway parody. Again, nothing to jump up and down about, and certainly a far cry from *Hamlet.* Down to two monkeys and not at all optimistic that I'm even going to get a single act of the play written before the weekend expires.

10:23 A.M.: When I am sure nobody is looking, I sneak into the lab and try a tiny piece of monkey meat. Gamy.

11:33 A.M.: I hear on the news that a chimpanzee was spotted in the park last night. Could this be Wally?

12:01 P.M.: Finally the monkeys are typing. They've been at it about forty-five minutes and seem to be concentrating pretty hard. I don't want to interrupt their work, of course, but I'm dying to see what they're writing. Think I'll head out to lunch.

2:58 P.M.: Long lunch. When I got back, the chimps were napping. I tiptoed into the lab and looked at what they were writing. It certainly looked like *Hamlet.* Upon closer examination, however, I realized that what I was reading was not *Hamlet* at all, but the second act of *Your Five Gallants,* by the lesser Elizabethan playwright Thomas Middleton. So frustrating!!! I yell at the chimps to get back to work. They are surly from being awoken and bare their teeth at me. Too bad! We have work to do!

3:12 P.M.: They are typing again, but when I look at it, it's just more gibberish. I don't know if they are doing this to punish me for waking them, or if they really don't know the difference between random typewritten characters and iambic pentameter.

5:09 P.M.: Bored.

6:22 P.M.: Dinner. I go to Subway and bring back extra sandwiches for the monkeys, which they greedily devour. As for me, I can't even choke mine down, as the stench of monkey is now overpowering. No more work has been accomplished in my absence. I hear on the radio that animal control has captured the chimpanzee and is trying to determine where it came from. I think about calling, but decide against it. These monkeys were not obtained through official channels, and I think there are pretty strict laws about that sort of thing.

7:00 P.M.: The monkeys are at work again, and I am afraid to interrupt.

9:02 P.M.: Binky and Tiny are wrestling (adorable). I sneak a look at their work. Binky has written a dirty limerick and what appears to be a passable translation of Cicero's *In Vaticinium*. While I am impressed with the quality of the translation, this gets us nowhere closer to having a completed copy of *Hamlet*. The only thing Tiny wrote is an incredibly tedious description of a solid brass locking mechanism. It is riddled with typographical errors, however, and B-O-R-I-N-G. We are quickly running out of time. The guys will be here to pick up their monkeys in less than three hours. I think about springing for more Red Bulls, but decide against it.

10:22 P.M.: I beg the monkeys to get back to work, but they have discovered the light switch and are going crazy with it.

10:39 P.M.: I place some bananas near the typewriters in the hopes that this will lure them back to work. Nope. They eat the bananas and then return to the light switch.

11:28 P.M.: A last flurry of activity. Binky and Tiny are hard at work, and I am not going to move a muscle until they are done. Hopefully, they will at least get some of *Hamlet* written before the weekend is over. A partial victory is better than none at all.

12:02 A.M.: The monkey guys just left. They were not *at all* happy when I told them about the dead bonobo (they already knew about Wally and he is back in their custody). They gave me a pretty good tongue-lashing, but my feeling is, if they didn't want the monkeys to kill and eat each other, they probably should have told me that was a possibility before entrusting them to my care. Needless to say, I lost my entire deposit. Great—there goes the money for my trip to Foxwoods.

After they left, I collected the monkey's final work. Most of it was, as usual, gibberish, but somebody made a very nice picture of a rose using only slash marks and ampersands. Also, they left me a gracious note thanking me for the sandwiches and for getting them out of the lab for the weekend. Whether or not they understood what they were writing or it was all just random typewriter marks is, again, a total mystery. But I have to believe that even if they didn't know *exactly* what they were saying, there was at least some sort of primitive attempt to communicate.

What did I learn? When I started this experiment, I had my doubts. Could an infinite number of monkeys, given an infinite amount of time, produce *Hamlet*? If my abbreviated attempt to find out is any clue, I would have to say no. Cicero? Yes. Thomas Middleton? Without a doubt. But Shakespeare is widely considered to be the greatest writer in history, and *Hamlet* is one of his greatest works. To expect a monkey, even an infinite number of monkeys, to be able to reproduce that level of genius is probably asking a bit much. Perhaps one of his minor works like *The Winter's Tale,* or a couple of sonnets, but *Hamlet,* with its themes about the complexity of action, and even the nature of existence itself?

I doubt it.

Next weekend: I'll see how long I can hold my breath.

Job Orientation

HI, have a seat. I'm Debbie. I'm the manager here, and I will be conducting your orientation today. On your application, you wrote that you're looking for a challenging position in retail sales. Well, I think we can guarantee you that. "Challenging" is pretty much our modus operandi around here. Even in our busy season, we sometimes have a difficult time moving merchandise, but I suppose that's to be expected in a store that sells nothing but dead fetuses preserved in decorative jars.

You're probably asking yourself when exactly it is I'm referring to when I say our "busy season." You got me. We don't have one. Although we do notice a slight uptick in sales right before Halloween.

Okay, so. The job is pretty straightforward. All new associates start out as greeters. That means you stand at the front of the store and when people come in, you say, "Hi, welcome to Baby in a Jar." That's it. Our more senior associates will take it from there.

During downtime, and believe me, there's *a lot* of downtime, I ask that you keep all the display jars dusted. We've also got an aromatherapy cartridge that needs to be changed twice a day. For some reason, our research department has concluded that the scent of fresh-baked apple pie makes people more inclined to buy babies in jars. Why that is, we don't know, and frankly we don't care. It's definitely an improvement over the way the store *used* to smell.

When it comes to sales, our basic philosophy is "Let the product sell itself." The thing is, when you're selling pickled fetuses in glass jars, people pretty much know up front whether they're interested in purchasing or not. This is not the kind of store that gets a lot of "impulse buyers," so mostly we're just there to expedite their decision-making process. We don't do a lot of "hard selling." We tried it in the past, and frankly, people felt it was in bad taste.

Maybe you want to know why in the world anybody would want to buy what we have to sell. The truth is, people will buy anything for the right price. And through exhaustive market research, we've learned that the right price is $49.95.

A quick word about dress. Although we don't have a uniform, we do ask all of our associates to dress "business casual," and we prefer women to wear skirts that extend to the knee. This is because a significant percentage of our clientele describe themselves as "Fundamentalist Christians," who I'm told use our products in certain kinds of protests, and also as gifts.

I should stress that Baby in a Jar does not subscribe to any particular religious or ideological agenda. The only thing that unites all of our customers is their desire to purchase a baby in a jar.

Actually, although we will continue to sell our product just the way it is, we are increasingly finding that our jars are just as popular, or even more popular, than the fetuses. Some of our customers buy the baby in a jar, and then get rid of the baby. We call it "throwing the baby out with the bathwater," but that's just a joke between us. Please don't share that one with our customers.

FYI, if anybody asks, it's not bathwater; it's formaldehyde.

People often ask us about our history. In 1994, our founder noticed that he could not find a one-stop source for fetuses in handblown crystal jars and goblets. Rather than complain about the situation, he saw it as an opportunity. One year later, our first (and to date only) Baby in a Jar location opened.

Maybe you're wondering why we don't sell any other products. It's a good question, and one we get a lot. Our founder believes that our mission is to do one thing and to do it better than anybody else. It might surprise you to learn that since we opened for business, Baby in a Jar has been the unequivocal leader in the recycled fetus category every single year. That's a distinction we wear with honor.

Listen to me running off at the mouth. Please forgive me. Like all of our associates, I take a lot of pride in what we do here at Baby in a Jar. Because at the end of the day, I believe that even though it's the babies in jars that get people *into* the store, it's the people *outside* the jars who keep them coming back.

Anyway, welcome. The benefits here are great and all of our associates get a 10 percent discount on store merchandise, which may not sound like a lot, but believe me, it really adds up over time.

This Is How I Party

YOU know that song "Everybody's Working for the Weekend"? That's my theme song.

All week I've got my nose to the grindstone, but from Friday at 5:01 P.M. until Monday at 8:59 A.M., I am officially "on swerve." Nobody parties with more intensity or focus than me. For some people, partying is what you do to unwind. Not me. For me, parties are my creative outlet. Parties, for me, are serious fun.

How do I party?

With exuberance.

With ferocity.

With a fierce desire to win.

What does it mean to "win" at a party? It means having the BEST time, eating the MOST canapés, throwing up the MOST throw-up. It means showing up alone, but going home with the HOTTEST girl who is the LEAST conscious. *That's* how you win.

This was my weekend:

After work on Friday, I put on my Axe body spray and headed out to begin my warm-up foray into the dark heart of party. I started at T.G.I.F.'s.

"Party of one?" the hostess asked.

"Not for long," I responded.

Within minutes, the hostess and her two smokin' friends were sharing a heapin' plate of potato skins with me and alternately downing copious amounts of peach liqueur. Potato skins and peach liqueur? Maybe it's not a combination you're familiar with. That's because it's expert-level partying. The kind they do on the Greek island of Mykonos. And trust me, once you've gone Greek, there's no lookin' back. Unless it's her back you're looking at while you're drilling her and her two friends in the employee's break room at T.G.I.F.'s, which is what I was doing about twenty minutes after I arrived.

The night was still young when I finished, so I drove over to Applebee's to see what was cooking over there. Turns out A LOT! The game was on, and I'm not talking about the football game on TV. I met a couple of honeys who had a taste for the finer things in life. Like nachos and my dick.

After Applebee's, it was over to Bennigan's for some late-night shenanigans. At this point, I was no longer hungry, but my whistle needed some wetting. I ordered a couple of shots of Jägey, and then did my thing with a divorcée who was looking for a little do-re-mi. We hit the dance floor HARD. Creed was on the stereo, and I got a little crazy when lead singer Scott Stapp told me to take it higher. I did. Higher, longer, and harder. It was all I could do to keep it in my pants. So I didn't. I twirled it around like a baton and let the majorettes fight over it. Which they did. ALL. NIGHT. LONG. T'wasome! (Shorthand word I invented for "It was awesome.")

Saturday was pretty much a repeat of Friday. Only instead of T.G.I.F., the Bee, and Benny G's, it was Houlihan's, the Cheesecake Factory, and Chili's. And instead of hostesses, honeys, and a divorcée, it was a kindergarten teacher, a nun, and some dude named Larry. Plus a round of minigolf with the kid I mentor. And that was just the morning. The afternoon and evening were even SICKER.

Lunch was at the Olive Garden, where I got my breadstick dipped in a juicy dish of olive oil. I followed that up with a double order of tiramisu (in this case, not a euphemism for sex), topped off with a cordial consisting of one part brandy, one part peppermint schnapps, and three parts black chick riding my cock. Then it was on to Planet Hollywood at the Cherry Hill Mall for my weekly Saturday night blowout. The Planet spun a little groovier that night, let me tell you. If you've never done it on top of Herbie the Love Bug, you don't know what it means to live. (Unfortunately, I found out later in the week that I contracted my own "love bug" that night. Nothing a strong course of antibiotics won't fix.) I may not be as famous as some of the celebs who usually visit Planet Hollywood, but I definitely made my mark. All over Harry Potter's cape.

Sunday was a blur. IHOP, Chuck E. Cheese's, Dave and Buster's, the library, the Hard Rock Cafe, Perkins, my mom's house, Sea World, the Ground Round, Larry's house, Wrigley Field, your mom's house, the Space Needle, every brew pub in the world, outer space, Houlihan's again, and of course, what weekend would be complete without a stop at Hooters?

Hooters: party Mecca. A lot of people think Hooters' best days are behind it. Not me. The brew is still cold, the wings are still hot, and the conversation is still sparkling. There is a misconception that Hooters Girls are vacuous sex objects. Not at all. Most of them are ambitious college students simply paying their way through school, and if you get to know them as I have, you will discover they are as extraordinary and varied as all the world's butterflies. So yes, I go to Hooters for the conversation. And the Jell-O shots. And the fucking.

The weekend ended at exactly 8:59 A.M. Monday, at my desk, in my cubicle, with a spreadsheet in front of me. Believe me, I did a lot of spreading on a lot of sheets that weekend. And a lot of thinking. Thinking about how incredible it is to live in a country where you can live free and party to win. The weekdays might be tedious—after all, I can only save so many refugees doing my job at the UN—but the weekends? T'wasome.

A Suicide Note

BY the time you read this, I will be dead. Please don't blame yourself. It isn't your fault. The fault lies entirely with me. I am a failure as a husband, father, amateur astronomer, and crossword puzzle enthusiast. My haircut is out-of-date, my taste in music is terrible, and I recently discovered that those khaki pants I always thought were pretty cool are, in fact, not cool at all.

Further, I have always felt bad about all that nipple hair I have. It's not normal, and no matter how many times I pluck it, it always returns. Obviously, nipple hair is no reason to kill yourself, but when you think about it, nor is it much of a reason to live.

My career, too, has been a lifelong disappointment. As a young man, I dreamed of doing great things with my life. Never did I imagine I would spend twenty-three years as a quality-control manager for disposable pens. Do you have any idea how dispiriting it is to show up for work every day checking the quality of a product that was specifically designed to be thrown away?

In fact, I am writing this note with one of those very pens. There's a certain irony there, no? Writing a suicide note with a disposable pen? There is also a certain irony in the fact that the ink keeps getting clogged.

Also, I have a confession to make. Even though you forgave me for the affair I had with Katerina all those years ago, I feel the need to confess to you now that there was never any affair. The love notes that you found in that old shoebox were written by me. The lipstick you discovered on my undershorts was applied by me. And all those nights I said was working late? I was working late. The truth is, I don't even know anybody named Katerina, except for that girl who used to groom the dog, and we both know she considered me a bad tipper.

I guess I just wanted you to think of me as the kind of man capable of having a passionate international relationship with a much younger Swiss lingerie model. Looking back on the incident now, and taking into consideration your mocking laughter and taunts, I wonder if perhaps you suspected the entire affair was fiction all along.

Of course, I worry about Gary Jr. and how this will affect him. At first, I assumed it would be a terrible blow, but now I'm questioning this assumption, as I think back to all the times he said to me, "I wish you were dead." Many children say hurtful things like this, and I used to think he was just going through a teenage phase, but he's almost thirty years old now, and he still says it all the time.

I have always felt terribly about the incident we had with the telescope when Gary was a boy, and even though everybody agrees his eye patch looks very becoming, I still believe he harbors a certain amount of anger toward me. Please tell him (again) that I never thought he'd actually point it at the sun when I told him to; I just (foolishly) assumed he would know that was a bad idea. My sense of humor was always on the dry side—obviously, a little too dry for a seven-year-old boy.

As an aside, and despite what the tests showed, I still think Gary Jr. is a little stupid. Please don't tell him I said so, but I just wanted to be on record. I mean, it was obvious to everybody else that I was joking when I said he should point the telescope at the sun and stare. Everybody else found the remark very funny.

Regardless of whose fault it was, it was a tragedy. As was the time Pickles died. Yes, it was my fault that the dog got stabbed, but it was not my fault that the dog puked on the carpet. Had the dog not puked on the carpet, I feel pretty confident I would not have stabbed the dog. Let's agree to split the blame for this one between Pickles and myself fifty-fifty. Deal?

Another regret: our whale-watching honeymoon to Maine. I have always regretted that I said the whales reminded me of you. It was my dry sense of humor doing the talking, and I now realize it was a mean-spirited thing to say, even if it was more or less true. The unceasing follow-up jokes about your weight certainly didn't improve your mood, and perhaps if I hadn't made them, you wouldn't have barricaded yourself in the hotel bathroom that night and for most of the following week. Our relationship certainly seemed to take a turn for the worse after that incident, and I am sorry.

Sending you all those brochures for fat camp was probably not as funny as it was intended to be either.

Anyway, I have tried my best not to leave a mess. I spread a sheet (not one of the good ones) on the floor, and I put on an extra pair of underwear in case there is any postmortem unpleasantness related to my bladder, which as you know certainly gave me plenty of unpleasantness during life.

My will is in my top drawer, next to the pinch pot Gary Jr. made me for Father's Day that time. I saved it all these years even though it clearly portrayed me with devil's horns. I kidded myself into thinking he was being ironic, but now I'm not so sure.

Looking to the future, I hope one day you will remarry somebody terrific and forget all about me. Perhaps you will come to think of our time together the same way people think about one of my pens: somewhat useful while in their possession, instantly forgotten afterward.

Stan the Oracle

YOU may ask one question.

It may concern the past, present, or future. Perhaps you wish to know of love lost or gained. Maybe you seek professional guidance. Some have sought my knowledge to attain enormous wealth. Still others have desired only to help their fellow man. My job is not to judge, only to provide the information you seek.

There is nothing I do not know.

Almost all who seek my knowledge invest many years in simply finding me. Most never reach me at all. They either forfeit the search or die in the quest. Very few ever reach my door.

And now you have come, as I knew you would. Although, to be honest, I actually expected you a little later, which is why I am still in my bathrobe. I apologize. Normally I'm up at seven, but the battery on my alarm clock is out. I asked my wife, Sheila, to replace it, but she was so wrapped up in that stupid TV show she watches that she forgot. Long story short, I overslept, which screwed up my whole day, and on top of everything, you're a little early, and now I'm sitting here in my bathrobe like a schnook.

Consider your question with great care. You may only ask one. No follow-ups. This isn't like a White House press conference. You may not, for example, ask, "Is there a God, and if there is, does He like speedboats?" That's two questions. (But for the record, God thinks speedboats are great.)

Knowledge such as I possess is an amazing gift and a terrible burden. On one hand, the mysteries of the cosmos are laid bare before me. On the other hand, I have been robbed of life's greatest pleasure—discovery. For example, remember how everybody was so freaked out by that amazing plot twist in *The Sixth Sense*? Not me. I saw it coming.

Forget having a social life. Friendships are impossible, and romance is just pointless. Sheila is my third wife, and I can tell you right now that we're not going to make it.

In March, the cable is going to go on the fritz. I will offer to fix the cable, and we will quarrel because she will say she'd rather have an expert look at it. I will say I *am* an expert—I'm an expert in everything. She will roll her eyes and mutter under her breath in a mocking tone, "I'm an expert at *everything*." Then she will think about our lovemaking, and say, "That's a laugh."

The man who comes to fix the cable will be named Mitch. Married. One child. He and Sheila will begin a tempestuous affair consummated one evening while I'm at bingo night. Within a week, Sheila will leave me. Her parting words will be, "Bet you didn't see THIS coming, Smart Guy," and I will not bother replying.

Mitch will leave his family, and he and Sheila will move in together. Things will start to go south almost immediately.

One night, they will get into a fight about his habit of picking the dead skin off his feet and eating it. Things will get heated, and he will shoot her. Then he'll turn the gun on himself.

Of course, I could tell her all of this and prevent the whole thing, but I'll probably just keep my mouth shut because I can be kind of a prick like that.

I can see you're getting impatient. You have traveled a great distance and wish to ask me your question. Forgive me for being such a chatty Cathy this morning. I honestly don't know what's gotten into me today. I mean, I obviously literally know everything that's gotten into me; I'm just using a figure of speech.

The thing is that I rarely ever get a chance to talk to anybody, you know? To just sit and talk like normal people. It's a common problem among those in my profession. Yes, there are others like me. We are a small group, scattered across the globe. Once in a while we all get together for shits and giggles, but the truth is, it's worse being with those assholes than being alone. Talk about divas. Everybody thinks they're sooooo important. Plus, everything with them is such a production: I mean, try picking a restaurant with that group. Forget it. Also, when everybody already knows everything, what is there to talk about? Anytime anybody says anything, the inevitable response is, "I know."

I will say this, though—the dental plan is excellent.

A lot of us end up getting into booze or drugs or whatever. I tried sniffing glue for a while, but it gave me the spins. It's one of the weird ironies in my business—once you know everything, you spend most of your time trying to forget. It's impossible, of course, but you try. Sleeping helps. So does food. Those little Entenmann's donut holes? I could eat a whole box and not even notice. My thighs, on the other hand, definitely notice. I would ask if you think I look fat, but I already know the answer.

Lately, I've actually been thinking about getting a second job. Something to get my mind off *this* job, you know? Like delivering pizzas or something. I could do that. Think about it: I would never get lost, I would never forget the Crazy Bread. I think I would be really good at it. Maybe I'll do that. The only thing is, I'll have to be careful when I apply. I don't want them to think I'm overqualified.

Anyway, back to your question. And yes, I already know what you're going to ask, but I still need you to ask it anyway. It's kind of a formality.

Before you do ask, though, you've been very patient with me, so I'd like to give you a tip, gratis. You know that hairdresser you go to? Dawn? Trust me—and it doesn't take somebody who knows everything to tell you this—she's not doing you any favors. As I said, that one was on the house.

I know you're thinking about asking, "What is the meaning of life?" Don't waste your breath. Everybody wants to know the meaning of life, and honestly, I'm sick of telling people, so a few years ago I wrote down the answer on a piece of paper and printed up a whole mess of them at the copy shop. Feel free to take one on your way out.

And yes, that is a tip jar.

So, what do you want to know?

Lewis Black Hates Candy Corn: A Rebuttal

ON his 2007 Grammy Award–winning album, *The Carnegie Hall Performance* (which is not a pretentious name for a comedy album no matter what anybody says), Lewis Black spends over four minutes discussing candy corn. To summarize his opinion: he does not care for it.

Now, I like Lewis Black. I think he's a highly intelligent comedian who articulates a funny and cogent point of view often missing in today's overheated political rhetoric. When it comes to candy corn, however, he is a fucking idiot.

Were candy corn a person, it could sue for libel based on Mr. Black's vituperative commentary. Unfortunately, candy corn is not a person. (Although if it were, it would be the most delicious person in the world.) And so, it falls on me to give voice to the voiceless, to defend candy corn from Mr. Black's ad hominem attacks.

What follows is a point-by-point rebuttal based on the merits, or lack thereof, of Mr. Black's arguments. [A note: Although we share a surname, we are not related. In fact, I changed my name to Black from Schwartz. He, presumably, changed his name to Black from Fucking Idiot.]

He begins: "[Candy corn] does not taste like either candy or corn. It tastes like something that was made out of oil."

While good people can disagree about something as subjective as taste, I must take exception to his very first point. Candy corn does not taste like it was made out of oil. It tastes like it was made out of magic. That's how delicious candy corn is. If magic had a taste, it would be the sweet, slightly buttery taste of candy corn—as would rainbows, if they had a taste.

Furthermore, to argue that it tastes like neither candy nor corn is beside the point. No candy tastes like what it's supposed to represent. For example, there is a popular candy called Circus Peanuts, which is a candy representation of circus peanuts. For those of you who have never tried this particular candy, IT DOES NOT TASTE LIKE PEANUTS. When we want the taste of peanuts or corn, we eat peanuts or corn. When we want the taste of sunshine and smiles, we eat candy corn.

Candy is not limited to representations of vegetables and nuts. A popular bubble gum called Big League Chew is designed to replicate what actual baseball players put in their mouths—tobacco. Guess what? It does not taste like tobacco. Nor do candy cigarettes taste like real cigarettes. That's good news for parents who do not want their kids eating cigarettes.

"If you took all the bags of candy corn and melted them down, you could run a car."

Strangely enough, this is true. Candy corn is made, primarily, from sugar and corn syrup. So while candy corn does not taste like corn, it is made from corn. The same corn used to make ethanol, which, as I'm sure you know, "could run a car." This is where candy and science finally meet. Were you to melt down all those bags of sweetness and love, you would have a tremendous amount of potential energy to use for your driving purposes. Plus, your exhaust fumes would smell like leprechaun farts.

"It is one of the shittiest tastes I have ever had in my mouth."

Without having more information about what Lewis Black puts in his mouth, I can not rebut this.

"All the candy corn that was ever made was made in 1911."

I did a little research on this point. Candy corn was actually invented in the 1880s. As it happens, the 1880s were a boom time for inventors peddling their wares. The safety razor, motorcycle, trolley car, gasoline engine, contact lens, ballpoint pen, and handheld camera were all invented in this decade. If I had to rank these inventions in order of importance to humanity, where would I put candy corn? First? Of course not. Second? Yes.

Candy corn has brought more joy to humanity than all of those other inventions combined. Nobody ever slashed their wrists with candy corn. Nobody was ever involved in a candy corn pileup on the interstate. Nobody has ever taken compromising photographs with candy corn. Candy corn is all upside, no downside. When people talk about technology having a dark side, they are not talking about candy corn.

"They never had to make it again . . . we never eat enough of it."

Not true. Unfounded. Baseless. Disgusting. Did you know that total candy corn production in 2007 was three billion tons? That's an astonishing number! Where did I get that number? Simple. I made it up. But I did so to prove a larger point: people eat a lot of candy corn. On average, Americans eat four hundred pieces of candy corn a year. Again, I made that number up because even the mighty Google could not provide me with the information I needed to determine this figure. That doesn't mean it's wrong—it simply means it could be right!

"And so, literally, after Halloween, the candy corn companies send out their minions . . . and they go from garbage can to garbage can and collect the candy, and throw it back in the bags. And it appears next year."

When did Lewis Black become a communist? The reason I ask is, he obviously doesn't love America or its capitalist system, because a capitalist would know this rudimentary economic concept: supply and demand. There is obviously a demand for candy corn. There could be no candy corn companies were there not.

It follows that, since apparently "nobody" eats candy corn, companies that make the stuff could only exist, at least in Lewis Black's demented view of the universe, if they were subsidized. By whom? The government. What kind of government subsidizes candy companies? Simple. Communist governments.

Clearly somebody is eating the stuff—supply. And American know-how provides the demand. If Comrade Black prefers, I'm sure he can find a time machine somewhere that will provide him with a one-way ticket to the old Soviet Union, where I am told there used to be a constant and crippling candy corn shortage. I am also told that on those rare occasions when candy corn was available, good citizens waited in line for *hours* to get it, only to be disappointed when they finally reached the front of the line and were handed a pair of shoes.

"I will never forget the first time my mother gave me candy corn. She said, 'Lewis, this is corn. And it tastes like candy.'"

Lewis Black's mother hates her child. That's what I take from the above sentence. What kind of person would describe candy corn as "corn that tastes like candy"? Why didn't she describe it properly, like this: "Lewis, this is corn-shaped candy, and it tastes like magic."

I will reiterate my original point. If Lewis Black thinks that candy corn should taste like corn, he is utterly misguided. So much so that it makes me question whether or not he's even fully in control of his own mental faculties. Candy corn was never intended to taste like corn. It was intended to taste better.

And it does.

All candy tastes superior to its natural counterpart. This is why grapes are referred to as "nature's candy," but candy is not referred to as "humanity's grapes." Those are testicles.

In the 1984 comedy *Irreconcilable Differences*, a young Drew Barrymore attempts to divorce her parents. I only wish Lewis Black had seen this movie as a young man—perhaps he could have saved himself from a lot of torment. Or maybe

Social Services could have paid a little more attention to the Black household. There are some very good foster families out there. Good foster families, I should add, that do not hate America.

Why does Lewis Black have so much hatred for goodness? I do not know. Because I am not a trained psychologist, I think it would be unethical for me to attempt to analyze him. But based upon his feelings regarding candy corn, I think it is safe to assume that he hates freedom, hates himself, and wants to fuck his mother.

I No Longer Love You, Magic Unicorn

PLEASE sit down. Or stand. I guess standing is probably easier for you. This is so hard for me. These things always are, but we need to talk. I don't know how to say this, so I'm just going to say it. I no longer love you, Magic Unicorn.

These feelings have been building for a long time, and I can't even tell you exactly why I feel the way I feel. I just do.

Yes, we've had many good times together. Like when you took me to your home, Magic Unicorn Land, where we frolicked on clouds and ate cotton candy every day for breakfast. Or the time you made it snow in the middle of July. Do you remember how we had a snowball fight and tobogganed down Chestnut Hill? And even though I developed a pretty serious case of Lyme disease from that, it was worth it. And I can't even count the number of times you let me burrow my head into your downy unicorn mane when I was sad. We had many good times, and I will always remember you fondly for that.

So what happened? There's no one answer to that question. It's everything and nothing. It's the fact that you claim to be an expert at balloon tying, but when push comes to shove you have no balloon tying talents at all. You can't even hold the balloons in your unicorn hooves, magical or no. Yet if I even mention this fact to you, you explode at me. You have a temper, Magic Unicorn. You have a very bad temper.

Perhaps it's because you tease the dog so much. The dog never did anything to you, and yet you never miss an opportunity to provoke and goad him. Why? The dog was never a threat to our relationship. Maybe it was all in good fun for you, but I couldn't help but notice that when you took your sabbatical last year, the dog's shaking condition noticeably improved. When you returned, so did the shakes. Look, I know that a little competition between family pets is natural, but when one of those pets is magic, it's no longer a fair fight.

Or perhaps it's because you claim diplomatic immunity even though both of us know that diplomatic immunity does not apply to unicorns.

Or the fact that *somebody* peed on the drapes that time, and while you claimed you had nothing to do with it, I noticed that the pee was sparkly, and we both know there's only one creature in this house who has iridescent urine. I didn't want to confront you with this telling piece of evidence because I did not want to deal with your temper—or your specious claims of diplomatic immunity. So I just had the drapes cleaned and didn't say another word about it. But I have to say, the lying has become a problem.

Then there is the small matter of the rent. When we moved out of my parents' house, we agreed that you would pay a small portion of the rent. Obviously you are a unicorn and so you cannot be expected to hold down a job. On the other hand, you are magic, and so getting money should not be a problem for you. I can't help but notice that whenever the rent is due you plead poverty, and yet you always seem to have enough money for new ribbons for your horn and bows for your tail.

When I was younger, none of this stuff bothered me. The temper, the lying, the vanity. After all, I was the new kid in the neighborhood and I didn't have any friends until you came along. I was willing to overlook all of your flaws because you were funny and kind to me, and because you never made fun of my teeth.

But now I have grown older, my braces are gone, and frankly, for the past several years, I've been having a hard time even believing in magic unicorns. Maybe this is just a natural part of the maturation process. I don't know. All I know is that lately it has struck me as increasingly silly that a thirty-six-year-old man has a magic unicorn named Dewey.

I packed your things and put them by the door. Please don't look at me with those big magic unicorn eyes. The truth is, this is going to be better for you, too. We both know I haven't spent nearly as much time with you as I once did. But can you blame a guy for preferring to spend his free time with his fiancée instead of with an invisible magical horned horse? Can you honestly blame me?

Look, Dewey, you're going to be fine. I took out an ad in the *Pennysaver* last week. Turns out there's a boy across town whose parents just divorced, and he's in the market for a magic unicorn. I told him all about you, and we scheduled an interview at eleven. It's kind of far away, I know, but if you use your magical powers, I'm sure you can get there on time.

Some DJ Names I've Been Considering

RECENTLY I read a study with a conclusion that was, frankly, startling. By the year 2013, every man, woman, and child on earth is going to need a DJ name. Nowhere in the article was it explained *why* we would all need DJ names, but just because I don't understand the science behind the study doesn't mean it isn't true.

We've been in this situation before; scientists repeatedly warn us about impending danger, only to be ignored until it's too late. Well, I've learned my lesson. This time I'm getting ahead of the curve. I've already started considering potential DJ names so that when the time comes, I'll be ready.

• DJ Freaq: Any DJ name that ends in "q" is pretty cool. The problem with this one, though, is that I think "freaq" is a little hard to pronounce at first glance. (I pronounce it "Freak," just with a "q" instead of the "k.") Might people think it's pronounced "Free-Q"? That would be terrible. This is the same reason I have never liked the singer Sade. If I can't pronounce your name right off the bat, chances are I'm not going to like your music either. Maybe DJ Freaqy would be better, but then I lose the "last letter q" thing, which was the whole point.

- DJ Animal Lover: This also has some pros and cons. On the plus side, I like that it takes social activism to the realm of the DJ. You don't often find DJs making a social statement with their DJ names. "Animal Lover" is a little clunky to say, though, and it's also (let's be honest) a little gay.

- DJ Super DJ: This one's very good because it's almost a palindrome. Also, it's kind of funny, which is good because chances are, when I'm finally up there "spinning the wheels of steel," I'm going to pick more than my fair share of Weird Al. It's good to tip people off that there's going to be a lot of Weird Al ahead of time, so they're not too disappointed when I fade from Kanye West to "Eat It." This one definitely makes the short list.

- DJ VD PHD: This one also makes the short list. I like that it's all initials. DJ = Disc Jockey. VD = Venereal Disease. PHD = I don't know what PHD stands for, but it makes me sound intelligent. Put it all together and you get a very smart DJ who likes to fuck. Smart and sexy is a difficult combination to beat in a DJ name. Potential drawback: it's kind of a tongue twister.

- DJ Sandra Bullock Fan: Honestly, this one probably doesn't have much of a shot, but Sandra Bullock doesn't get nearly the credit she deserves as an actress and person. Everything I read about her in *US* and *People* makes me really, really like her. Even so, there might be a better platform for me to express my admiration for the star of *Miss Conge-*

niality 2: Armed & Fabulous than in my DJ name. And yet, there might not be.

- DJ Shake Your Rumplestiltzkin: Another good choice. It definitely puts one in the mind of sweaty tushies, which is a bad thing in the corporate world but a very good thing in the world of underground after-hours dance clubs that specialize in postmodern trance hop. So it's good, but I wonder if it reads a little too "urban"?

- DJ Bertolt Brecht: A DJ could do a lot worse than naming himself after one of the twentieth century's most important playwrights and dramaturges. Might be a little obtuse.

- DJ LOL: If "friendly and computer literate" is the image I decide to project as a DJ, this would be a fine choice. On the other hand, will it seem dated in 2013?

- DJ Edamame: Rhythmically, this is excellent. Kind of rolls off the tongue. And I really do enjoy edamame, which are boiled and salted soybeans. Plus, Japanese names always sound awesome. Short list.

  Some other names I'm considering:

- DJ Sweaty Goat
- DJ Nipples
- DJ Sweaty Goat Nipples
- DJ Your Mama's on Zoloft
- DJ Arlene Zambrowski
- DJ Herpes
- DJ Cake Tastes Good Unless It's Dry
- DJ Don't Talk Shit About Allah

Obviously I have my work cut out for me. This is why it's critically important to get under way *now,* before it's too late. Also, I want to make sure to get a cool DJ name before all the good ones are snapped up. DJ names are like snowflakes: each is unique. There can only be one "DJ Sandra Bullock Fan" after all, and it would be a shame if some kid in Bangladesh got it while I dithered.

Am I taking a risk by publicizing my short list now? Yes, but I'm doing it for humanity's sake. Not my own. We've *got* to get DJ names. Now! Ignoring this gathering storm will only make it worse in the long run. If you thought global warming was bad, just wait until 2013. It'll be like Hurricane Katrina, the tsunami, and a hit of really bad E all rolled into one.

I Have an Indomitable Spirit

I have an indomitable spirit. Nothing gets me down. Perfect example: the other day, I got into a little fender bender. I was backing out of the driveway and smacked right into the paperboy. The car was badly dented. Now a lot of people would look at that dent and be upset. Not me. Because instead of focusing on how badly damaged my car was, all my attention went to that poor paperboy and how badly damaged he was. Compared to that boy, the damage to my car was nothing.

By concentrating on the positive (the minor damage to my automobile vs. that broken, crumpled boy), I ended up feeling much, much better. In fact, I felt so good that I didn't give the incident another thought as I got back into my car and sped off to work. Later that day, when one of my coworkers asked about the damage to my car, I just smiled and said, "Oh that? That's nothing. You should have seen the *other* guy!" Of course my coworker thought I was joking, and we had ourselves a good old-fashioned chuckle. You see how I used my personal tragedy to brighten somebody else's day? That's the hallmark of an indomitable spirit.

Incident at the Torpedo

LET'S start from the top, shall we? Name? Is that two "l"s or one? Alan. Is that right? And I assume the last name is like the color? With an "e." Alan Greene. Very good.

So, Mr. Greene, what brings you to Six Flags today?

Of course you do, sir. It's a free country, and you have the right to go anyplace you like. The only reason I ask is, as I'm sure you noticed, you don't fit the profile of our normal customer base. No offense, of course, but normally our guests are a little bit younger. Do you mind if I ask how old you are?

Eighty-one years old. Well, that's very impressive, Mr. Greene, very impressive indeed. Did you come to the park alone today?

You did. I see. Okay, let's talk about the incident. Would you like to tell me your version of what happened?

You got on line for the Torpedo, right.

I understand it was a long line, sir, and we're very sorry about that. The Torpedo, as I'm sure you know, is our newest attraction. Might I add, I think it's also our most exhilarating attraction. Consequently, the lines have been long, which is an unfortunate fact. What happened next?

It *is* hot. I definitely agree with you there. That's why

we've placed spray misters all over the park. Those misters can be a real lifesaver on a day like today. I don't mean that literally, of course, although a man of your advanced age might think twice before standing on a line like that in this kind of heat.

You took off your shirt. Perfectly understandable. No sir, that's not a problem at all. Many of our guests prefer to forgo shirts, especially during this time of year. I probably would have done the same thing myself. Between you, me, and the lamppost, those misters can only do so much. Okay. You're on line. The shirt comes off. How did you meet the lady in question? Did you initiate the conversation or did she?

You don't recall.

Okay, well according to the report I have from Nicole—that's the young lady's name—she says that you initiated the conversation. She says you complimented the tattoo on her back. Is that true?

I did see the tattoo, sir, and it is a fine piece of work. No sir, I don't, but if I did I would probably ask her where she got hers done, because that's as good a tattoo of a butterfly as I've ever seen, and as I'm sure you can imagine, I see quite a few of them working here. Although in my case, I probably would opt for something a little less feminine than a butterfly. Perhaps a bulldog, which is the mascot of my alma mater. "Go bulldogs!" That's not really relevant right now, of course. Why don't you continue with the story.

You don't recall what happened next. Okay. I'm just going through my report here. Nicole says she thanked you for complimenting the tattoo, then turned back to her friend,

Tanya. Incidentally, Tanya corroborated Nicole's version of the events for what it's worth. What happened next?

Well, Mr. Greene, that is decidedly at odds with Nicole's version of the events. She says the next thing that happened was that you asked if she would, and I'm quoting here, "like to see your junk."

No sir, I'm not calling anybody a liar. I'm merely trying to ascertain what occurred. She says you asked if she would like to see your junk, to which she replied, "No."

No sir, she did not mention that she called you a "creepy old perv." I'm jotting that down as we speak. Creepy. Old. Perv. Got it.

After that, Nicole says she turned back to her friend again, and within a few moments she says she felt, and again I'm quoting, "something furry like a caterpillar" on her back. She says she tried wiping it off, but it kept returning. Finally she turned around, and when she did, she says she saw you rubbing her shoulder blade with your nipple. Do you dispute that?

Okay, let's hear your version.

Yes, I understand it was crowded. As I said, the Torpedo is our newest attraction, so yes, I can see how people might be jostling each other in line. When you put it that way, I can absolutely see how it might be possible for a shirtless man to accidentally rub his nipple on the shoulder blade of the person in front of him. The problem I'm having, though, is Nicole says, and again this is corroborated by Tanya as well as two gentlemen who observed the entire incident, that you were pinching your nipple at the time and making, quote "goo goo noises," which to my ears doesn't sound accidental. Can you understand why Nicole felt the need to call security?

I hope it was all a big misunderstanding, Mr. Greene, I really do, but here's the problem I'm having: when I combine furry nipple pinching with goo goo noises it starts to sound less and less like a misunderstanding and more and more like a creepy old perv, which I believe is the phrase Nicole used. We simply can't have our guests groping each other, Mr. Greene.

Of course I have, sir. Many times. But there's a difference. When other people do it, it's consensual. That's the distinction I'm forced to make here. Consensual groping, while possibly distasteful to some, is still legal—within certain boundaries, of course. Your behavior, however, really crosses the line, sir. Even if it had been consensual, which clearly it was not.

Yes sir, I have a grandfather about your age. My grandmother died several years ago, so I definitely can see how lonely an older man can get. I tell you what my grandpa does: he plays slot machines with some of the ladies from his church group. Now that may not be as exciting as shooting down a sixty-five-degree incline at eighty miles an hour like on the Torpedo, but he seems to like it, and he's made some very good friends that way. So yes, I can understand how a man of your advanced age might crave female companionship. But I have to say, in my opinion, Six Flags is probably not the most appropriate venue for you to find that companionship.

Yes, I understand that you have a season pass, and yes, I understand that you want to get your money's worth, but I hope you can understand my position. We simply can't have our older guests making unwanted advances at our younger guests. Now I've spoken to Nicole and she is willing to forgo pressing charges if you are willing to forgo that season pass of yours. Otherwise, I'm afraid I'm going to have to get law enforcement involved, and that wouldn't be good for anybody, would it?

Yes, I'm sure you did serve your country, Mr. Greene, and we're all very grateful for that, but I'm afraid that's neither here nor there at the moment. No sir, I have no idea what they did to you in Korea. But again, I have to say, that's not relevant to this discussion.

It's really your choice about how you would like to proceed from this point forward.

No, I'm afraid you won't be able to return to the park this season. In fact, I'm afraid we're going to have to ask you never to return again.

Thank you, Mr. Greene. I think that's the best decision for everybody. Thank you, sir. I like it, too. Yes, my wife got it for me for Christmas last year. It is silk, yes. Please stop touching my tie, Mr. Greene. No, I don't want to see your junk.

I'm going to ask Dave to escort you out now.

Good Skiing Form

SKIING is a lot of fun and great exercise, but to really enjoy the sport to its fullest, skiers must always use good form. What is good skiing form? Some people think it means bending at the knees and keeping the elbows tucked. Bent knees and tucked elbows are important, yes, but good skiing form takes a lot more than that. It's an attitude, a hearty can-do spirit that's as much mental as it is physical. What follows are a few tips I've come up with to ensure that your time on the mountain is as safe and fun as possible.

- Stay hydrated! People often think that if it's not hot outside you can't get dehydrated. Guess again, stupid. Cramping can turn a bunny hill into a double-black-diamond date with death. If you find yourself getting thirsty, don't wait until you happen upon a mountain stream. By then it will be too late. Instead stop, drop, and scoop. Stop where you are, drop to the ground, and scoop as much snow into your mouth as you can. Sure, you might get some funny looks, but you'll be the one laughing when they are dead on the mountain while you're kicking back with a cup of fruit salad at the lodge.

- Keep your eyes open! It may be tempting to try to emulate those heroic blind skiers you see on mountains all over the world, but remember that those skiers aren't blind by choice. Their blindness is due either to a bizarre genetic abnormality or maybe some kind of weird mutation like in *X-Men*. These people don't ski blind because they want to "look cool" or "look blind." They do it because they have no other choice. For them it's either ski blind or don't ski at all. If you still feel the need to limit your sight, a challenging alternative to total blindness is to wrap a colorful bandana around your eyes before heading down the hill. Not only will you look like you're in Aerosmith but it also has the added benefit of warming the eyes on a chilly day.
- Don't ski horny! This tip will no doubt elicit a couple of chuckles. That's okay, go ahead and get it out of your system. Then read up, because this tip could save your life. Skiing horny is not only distracting but it can also upset your center of gravity. Why? Because boners weigh more than limp dicks. Gentlemen, make sure you are fully flaccid before attempting to ski, ESPECIALLY ON MOGULS! If you find yourself with a raging hard-on at the ski lodge, ask a bathroom attendant to help. Generally these foreigners will happily "finish you off" for a modest tip. Plus, they usually clean up any resulting mess. If you can get past the awkwardness of the situation, it will be the best (and safest) three dollars you ever spend.
- Ski tipsy, not drunk! Time and again, I see people getting paralyzed and killed on the slopes. Sometimes they get paralyzed, then killed. Sometimes killed, then paralyzed.

The reason? Too much booze. Everybody knows that a couple of relaxing drinks before skiing is to be commended. Drink too much, though, and you will ski off a cliff, EVEN IF THERE ARE NO CLIFFS AROUND! The trick is knowing your limit. One simple test—go to the top of the mountain and ski down in a totally straight line. If you find yourself swerving all over the place, chances are you've had too much. If that's the case, stop, drop, and scoop. Get some of that invigorating cold snow into your system as soon as possible; too much alcohol can instantly transform a pleasant day on the slopes into a blunt-force traumatic brain injury. Skiing high is fine.

- The ski patrol is not there for your amusement! Yes, they have zippy snowmobiles and sleds, but that doesn't mean they want to spend their day speeding up and down the mountain responding to fake emergencies just because you find it amusing to lie on the snow screaming, "I think I broke my neck!!!" And never tell the ski patrol there's been an outbreak of Ebola on the trails. They won't find it funny, and neither will anybody else. Ebola is never a laughing matter—not even on vacation. The ski patrol are trained professionals with washboard abs and totally ripped bods. As an aside, some of them like to do it in the hot tub.

- Funny blow-up sumo costumes are a no-no on the slopes! Yes, they are a great way to meet people. Yes, they are hilarious. But even the safest blow-up sumo costumes were not designed for skiing. That technology is still years away from becoming a reality. Blow-up sumo costumes impede mobility and worse, they reinforce negative stereotypes about the Japanese. Japanese people have enough problems without seeing their culture mocked by insensitive winter sportsmen. Some great alternatives to funny blow-up sumo costumes include outrageous Dr. Seuss–style hats, furry clip-on animal tails (also good to offset any additional "boner weight"), Jimmy Carter masks, or my favorite, funny blow-up Chinese laborer costumes.

- Some other little tips: swim flippers aren't a good substitute for skis, don't ask for horseradish at the lodge (they won't have it and it pegs you as an amateur), and try to use the term "après-ski" as much as possible.

Skiing is a great wintertime sport that can be enjoyed by people of both sexes, all ages, and most races. Take it from me, if you follow my advice on good skiing form, you're guaranteed to have a great time on the slopes. If you don't, you might still have a great time. But you also might end up a vegetable.

An Open Letter to the Hairstylist Who Somehow Convinced Me to Get a Perm When I Was in Sixth Grade

Dear Geoffrey of Geoffrey's Hair Creations,

You son of a bitch. I didn't have the nerve to call you that when I was twelve, but now I am a man so let me say it loud and clear: you, sir, are a son of a bitch.

As if I wasn't unpopular enough. As if I wasn't already routinely subjected to ridicule and torment due to my smallish stature, unconventional attire (top hat and tails), and, as one teacher put it, "counterproductive" personality. As if all of that wasn't enough, you had to go and add a synthetic Jewfro to my list of problems?

You son of a bitch.

I will give you credit, Geoffrey: you were sneaky. You never used the actual word "perm," suspecting perhaps that I would balk. Instead, you suggested that I might improve my appearance somewhat if I added some "wave" to my preternaturally straight hair. "Wave" conjures images of St. Tropez; I envisioned myself sunning on some beach, sipping a (nonalcoholic) daiquiri and regaling a bevy of topless socialites with my tales of triumph over Ms. Pac-Man.

And so I acquiesced—never suspecting that an hour later I would stand up from your beauty chair looking like the long-lost love child of Mr. Spock and Little Orphan Annie.

Instantly, I knew I had made a colossal error in judgment, which was confirmed by my mother, who told me I looked "adorable." Adorable is not how one wants to look at twelve, when the rest of his male classmates are sprouting armpit hair and the beginnings of mustaches. Besides, I did not look adorable. I looked like I had a sponge on my head. Nor did I want to look adorable. I wanted to look feral.

As bad as my new hairdo looked, it smelled worse. Like burned plastic rubbed in pool water. The smell burned my eyes and no amount of shampoo would wash it away.

Perhaps the fault is not entirely yours. Perhaps some of the blame rests with my mother, who, upon entering your salon, asked, "What do you suggest?" Perhaps she shouldn't have heeded your advice, even though my mother is a lesbian with about as much fashion sense as the handyman character Al from *Home Improvement*.

But I cannot entirely absolve myself from blame either. After all, I was twelve years old, old enough to know that the Strawberry Shortcake look was not going to go over well at my school.

Looking back on it now, it seems like *everybody* got a perm at Geoffrey's Hair Creations. The "creations" were, in fact, perms. Maybe that was the only thing you knew how to do, Geoffrey. Maybe you only attended the beauty academy on the day they were teaching the class about how to make smelly, curly hair.

Or maybe you are simply a specialist. A cardiologist is a heart specialist, maybe you're a perm specialist. But I suspect you're simply just a terrible hairstylist and a terrible person. And, as I said, a son of a bitch.

The perm took about six months to fully grow out. In that time, I recall not being picked for *either* hockey team during gym class, bursting into tears during English class, being stood up by the only two people I had invited to my birthday party, and learning the word "faggot."

Was all of that your fault? No. Most of it, yes, but not all.

Sixth grade was never going to go well for me, no matter how my hair looked. I know this now, Geoffrey. You only made a bad situation worse, the equivalent of throwing grease onto a kitchen fire. The house was always going to burn down—you just helped it burn down a little quicker. From those ashes, though, a new boy arose. A new boy, with straight hair and a winning attitude. A new boy who was, sadly, just as unpopular as the old one.

I drove through my hometown recently and saw that your place of business has closed. What happened? Did you retire? Did the business go under? Or, as I hope, did you die? You know, Geoffrey, there is a special room in Hell reserved for bad hairstylists. It is small and hot and it smells like perms.

Instructions for the Cleaning Lady

HI there. I hope you have a great time cleaning my house today. Sorry I couldn't be here in person to help you out on your first day, but I have a real job. (Just kidding!!!) Anyway, all the cleaning products are under the sink in the kitchen. Please use *only* the ones labeled "Cleaning Lady." The other cleaning products are for my collection.

If you get hungry, help yourself to anything in the fridge. Please think of my fridge as your personal hotel minibar. And like a minibar, I keep a full inventory with pricing next to the fridge. You can either leave cash or, if you prefer, I can deduct the cost of the food from your pay. Oh, and don't use the silverware. I don't want you to be tempted to steal it. (Just kidding again!)

Now I know there is a tremendous amount of pet dander everywhere. I apologize for that. You would think a fellow who doesn't own any pets wouldn't have this problem. All I can say is, sorry. Just vacuum up the cat hair and dispose of it. Please save all the dog hair.

You may have some questions about the incredibly realistic life-size female dolls in one of the upstairs bedrooms. Don't worry—it's not what it looks like (ha, ha). These dolls are for medical purposes. I am certified in training CPR and creating CPR "scenarios." Last night, for example, I created a scenario in which I would have to perform CPR in a Victoria's Secret store, which is why they are all dressed like that. If you could just give them all a light dusting and a thorough mouth cleaning, that would be great. Also, if you must move them, please call them by their names, which I wrote on their tummies.

Now, the master bathroom. Filthy? Yes. My fault? Yes. The windows don't open in there and there is no ventilation. My advice would be to hold your breath, clean as much as you can, run outside, take another deep breath, and then clean some more. Keep doing this until you figure out a way to get that place SPOTLESS! Believe me, I don't envy you; I wouldn't clean that bathroom. In fact, I haven't, which is why it looks like that. I guess it's true what they say—you people really *do* do the jobs nobody else wants.

The rest of the house is pretty straightforward. Have fun. Just so you know, there are tiny video cameras hidden throughout the house, so I will definitely know if you took anything (not kidding).

Sorry I didn't leave any money for you this week. All I had were hundreds.

How to Approach the Sensitive Question: Anal?

GENTLEMEN, this is a problem so many of us have experienced: how to ask a young lady if she likes it in the pooper. From my personal experience, if you simply ask your date (particularly if it's a first date), you're most likely going to be met with, at best, nervous giggles or, at worst, a steely gaze followed by a request to be let off the back of your bicycle.

Why is this? I believe it's because "society" frowns upon this form of intercourse, even though nine out of ten women prefer it. (Like most other facts in this book, I just made that up.) Why do I put "society" in quotation marks? Because what is "society"? It's you and me, and the only way we are going to change "society" is by taking an active role in dispensing with the embarrassment and shame of putting your wiener in some chick's butt.

How do we do this? As loving men, how do we approach the sensitive question: anal?

There are a couple of different methods. The most common is what I call "the accidental method." Simply put, you wait until you are about to have intercourse. Then, you "accidentally" put it in her rear end. When she says, "That's the wrong hole," you say, "There's nothing wrong about it." From that point, it should be obvious how she wants you to proceed.

I don't recommend this approach because it catches the lady off guard and if, for some reason, she does not want to proceed in the prescribed manner, it necessitates you either cleaning yourself off or "double dipping," which is not a good idea for hygienic reasons.

Another approach is the "finger twaddle." I call it that because "twaddle" is a very funny word. This is a multistage process. First, during foreplay, spend some time fondling her tush. If she responds positively, insert your pointer finger, a maneuver I call "the twaddle." Twaddle around in there a little. She likey? Great. Now, as you twaddle, whisper the following in her ear: "Roll over, baby." The rest should take care of itself.

Maybe you're one of those guys who likes to lay down the rules of the road before the evening progresses to coitus. As I mentioned before, simply posing the question in a straightforward manner rarely achieves the desired result. Instead, try asking in an indirect way.

Perhaps you've just enjoyed a romantic dinner together (I suggest Red Lobster). The evening is going well, and you suspect the two of you might end up in bed together later in the evening. Great. Here's what you do: order dessert. (If you take my suggestion of Red Lobster, I further suggest the Chocolate Wave.) When your Chocolate Wave arrives, spoon some of that gooey concoction into her mouth and say, "I wish this gooey concoction was my wang, and I wish your mouth was your butt." If she says, "I wish that, too," you'll know where you stand. If she says, "That's disgusting," you can easily say, "I was just kidding." Or, less convincingly, you could try, "I think you misunderstood me." But that's not the kind of thing that's easily misunderstood.

If this is still too direct, take her on a long walk through a nature conservancy or arboretum. While strolling among the flora and fauna, take her hand in yours and say something like, "I'm having a great time. I'd like to know everything about you." Women love to hear that. Next, ask her a series of utterly meaningless questions: "What are your hopes and dreams?" "Have you ever been in love?" "What's the worst tragedy that's ever befallen you?" Et cetera, et cetera. As you are "listening," slowly wrap your arm around her waist and slide your hand down to the small of her back. Continue talking until you decide the moment is right for an "over-the-pant finger twaddle." This is accomplished by lightly caressing her anus in a "sympathetic manner." How do you caress somebody's anus sympathetically? Brother, if I have to tell you that, you need more help than I can offer.

Another tactic I have found helpful in the past is the tried-and-true "I have a friend who . . ." scenario. The way this works is pretty self-explanatory. While talking, mention that you have a friend who would like to fuck her in the ass. If she asks who, say "You don't know him," then quickly follow up with, "Isn't that so funny?" If she says anything other than "That's disgusting," then I think you can safely assume that she will respond positively to those three magic words: "Roll over, baby."

As you can see, there is no one way to deal with this perpetually vexing situation. Instead, try a variety of the techniques outlined above. Trust your intuition. And if, by chance, you find yourself with a woman who doesn't like it in the rear, don't despair. While anal sex is an important consideration when considering a mate, it's important to know that it's not the only consideration. Remember, over time, even the tightest tush will wear out, but a warm heart never will.[*]

*I confined this essay to the heterosexual community, as I don't know the protocol for the other half, although I suspect the conversation usually goes something like this:

"Wanna ass fuck?"

"Yes, I do."

Do Not Buy Tundra from a Door-to-Door Salesman

IF a man comes to your door one day and offers to sell you five acres of prime undeveloped Arctic tundra, do NOT buy it! He will be persuasive, this man, as he tells you about the "stark beauty" of the land, the unspoiled views, the pristine ecosystem, the clarity of the stars on freezing moonless nights. Yes, he will be good, this man. He will be very good. But DON'T buy any tundra!

As I once did.

Yes, I fell for this man's pitch. Over my wife's strenuous objections, I bought five acres of Arctic tundra from a door-to-door salesman, thinking it would be the perfect place to build my dream home and raise my family. Boy, was I wrong.

Everything about the move was a disaster. In fact, just getting to our new homestead proved to be incredibly difficult. First we had to drive to the airport, take a plane to Canada, take a smaller plane to a smaller part of Canada, then take a car to the end of a road where we got on a dogsled for nine days, until we were almost to the North Pole.

The trip was taxing for all of us, but especially for my three-year-old daughter. Before we left Connecticut she refused to leave the house unless she could wear her flip-flops.

Needless to say, you don't want to get into an argument like that with a three-year-old—not when you're already late for your plane. So we let her wear the flip-flops. By the time we got close to the North Pole we were all regretting that decision.

When we finally reached the tundra, it was tough to figure out which five-acre lot was ours because, honestly, everything kind of looks the same up there. It was important to find the *correct* lot though, because we specifically paid extra for a corner lot. The lack of corners though made it tough to distinguish which site was ours.

Just then, our Inuit guide, Ra-ka', decided that it would be the perfect time to inform us that there was no place nearby to buy either juice boxes or veggie burgers. No veggie burgers? Was he kidding? It's not like we were asking for fancy tempe burgers or anything, just any kind of run-of-the-mill soy patties. But Ra-ka' said there was nothing like that up there and if we wanted veggie burgers we should have brought our own. (He said all of this in Inuit, which took a long time to translate, especially because our Inuit dictionary, inexplicably, didn't have an entry for "veggie burger.")

Needless to say, I was pissed. I specifically asked the door-to-door salesman if there were supermarkets nearby, and he said that while he didn't know for sure, he was pretty confident there was a twenty-four-hour gourmet grocery nearby, as well as a very good jazz-themed pizzeria and an espresso shop. Wrong! Wrong! Wrong! I don't know if he was misinformed or what, but there was nothing of the sort anywhere within a thousand miles. I could tell my wife was getting very upset about the situation, but when I asked her what was wrong, she just stared at me as if the entire predicament was *my* fault. *I* wasn't the one who said the kids needed to get out of the house more.

Ra-ka' took the dogsled and left us on what we thought was our five-acre corner lot. It was very cold. Fortunately, we were all expecting the cold since we had read up on the tundra before leaving home. So we knew enough to bring blankets and mittens. My blue jeans, however, quickly became stiff with condensation, making it almost impossible to walk. The kids had a good laugh watching Daddy walk around our homestead like a robot. They busied themselves in the snow (or "permafrost," as it's called up there) while my wife and I mapped out the ideal location for our dream house.

We decided on a flat parcel in the northwest corner of our acreage because there was a scrubby little bush there, which looked dead, but we thought maybe in the springtime it would come back to life and provide the house with some much-needed greenery. Of course, it was June, so I'm not sure when we thought spring would be arriving.

That night we slept under the stars. As promised, they were spectacular. They were hard to enjoy, however, because my daughter's blackened toes were hurting her so much that she kept letting out loud, annoying cries. My son was not much better, incessantly complaining about the cold and the lack of *SpongeBob SquarePants*. None of us got much sleep that night.

In the morning, the kids were hypothermic and bordering on delirium. I suggested a rousing game of volleyball to get everybody's blood circulating, but nobody was in the mood. The only thing anybody wanted to do was huddle and moan. Plus, I forgot to pack the volleyball.

Did we eventually build our dream house on that parcel of prime undeveloped Arctic tundra? No, we did not. Within a few days, we called it quits and were evacuated by a rescue helicopter. To her credit, my wife did not say "I told you so"—not even once.

In the end, my son lost some fingers, my wife also lost some fingers and a toe, my daughter spent some time in a medically induced coma, and I lost the twelve thousand bucks I gave to that shyster who sold me the tundra in the first place. I tried calling his company to get a refund, but the telephone operator said there was no listing for Number One First-Class Tundra Real Estate Group. Turns out I'd been had—I felt like a real sucker.

To anybody considering a similar purchase, I know the tundra sounds great, but it has got some real drawbacks: the inhuman cold, the lack of food and shelter, the absence of any jazz-themed pizzerias, et cetera. Unless you're an *extremely* rugged, childless individual with superior survival skills, I would stay away from the Arctic altogether. You can get the exact same effect in Minnesota without all the hassle.

DON'T TELL ME TO CALM DOWN!!!

FIRST of all, I'm calm. Let's get that out of the way right now. I am calm, I'm very calm. I'm so calm, I'm almost unconscious. My near lack of consciousness is due to both my preternaturally calm disposition and also the fact that YOU JUST REAR-ENDED ME IN THE FUCKING PARKING LOT!!!

Don't tell me to lower my voice and don't tell me to calm down. In a motor vehicle accident, whoever hits the rear of the other person's car is automatically at fault. Therefore YOU ARE AT FAULT!!! Yes, I was driving backward through the parking lot at a rapid speed. Yes, technically your car was not "on." That, however, does not mean that you are not at fault. If the front of your car hits the rear of my car, you are at fault.

And I demand recompense. Lots of recompense. Like maybe a million recompenses. My car is totaled and if you notice, I am now speaking with a lisp. I DID NOT LISP BEFORE!!!

I had a speech impediment, yes, but I don't think ANYBODY would have characterized it as a lisp. A sibilant "s," perhaps. But NOT A LISP. Now, though, I'm just full-on lisping. Do you have any idea how that is going to impact my job as a gym teacher??? High school kids DO NOT RESPOND WELL TO AUTHORITY FIGURES WITH LISPS!!! That has been well documented in, literally, thousands of professional journals.

What are you—blind or something? How did you manage to be sitting in a parked car in this lot while I was driving through it backward? Were you not looking? Did you not see me doing figure eights and donuts in my whipcar? Or were you simply too self-absorbed to turn on your engine and drive away from me as I barreled toward you at speeds in excess of forty miles an hour?

DON'T TRY TO TURN THIS AROUND ON ME!!! What difference does it make WHY I was driving like that? What possible difference does my motivation make now that the damage is done???

Yes, I'm asking about YOUR motivation in sitting there because YOU had the power to prevent this accident! But YOU chose not to. YOU chose to sit in your parking spot reading your newspaper while waiting for your wife to come out of the supermarket. WHAT KIND OF MAN LETS HIS WIFE DO ALL THE GROCERY SHOPPING, ANYWAY??? A CAVEMAN, THAT'S WHAT KIND!!!

How am I supposed to explain this to Gary? What do you mean, "Who's Gary?" THIS IS GARY'S CAR, YOU MORON!!! Do you think a professional high school gym teacher can afford a car this nice? NO!!!

Gary is my friend whose place I am house-sitting while he's in Argentina. It was a "kill two birds with one stone" kind of situation in which Gary needed somebody to watch his house while my wife was simultaneously throwing me out of mine. And Gary SPECIFICALLY told me NOT TO DRIVE HIS CAR. Because he said I am—and this is his word, not mine—"untrustworthy."

He said, "Doug, I DO NOT want you driving my car." And what did I say? I said, "Okay, Gary," because Gary is my friend and I respect his wishes.

So what did I do? This morning, as soon as Gary left, I got in his car and started driving it around. Backward. That way the mileage wouldn't show up on his odometer. And the reason I was doing donuts in the parking lot is because THIS CAR IS SO SWEET that it would be a crime if I DIDN'T do donuts!!! And then you had to park in that stupid parking spot and ruin everything.

Listen to me, guy. Here's what we're going to do. When the police get here, you're going to tell them the whole thing was your fault. Okay? That way, we're both covered.

What do you mean, YOU'RE not covered? You're not SUPPOSED to be covered! As I already explained, this whole thing is YOUR FAULT! So why not just sack up and take one for the team? What team? OUR TEAM!!! Doug and you. You and Doug. That team. I'm a gym teacher, so with all due respect, I think I know a little bit more about teams than you.

Look, I think we can both agree that you ramming into the back of my car was an unfortunate turn of events here today. And I think we can also both agree that one of us is going to have to take the fall. Here's the problem: not only do I not have permission to be driving this car but I also don't have an active driver's license. My license was suspended precisely because ANOTHER ASSHOLE BACKED INTO ME in this same parking lot about six months ago. So, even though THIS IS YOUR FAULT, I suspect law enforcement is going to look askance at my particular driving status.

So I'm sure you can see my problem. I'm kind of in a pickle here. I'm over a barrel. Frankly, I'm in a pickle barrel, which is why I need you to cover my ass. Now, lest you think you're doing all the giving and I'm doing all the taking, I am prepared to compensate you very generously for your consideration.

How? Well, as I said, I am a teacher of physical education at a public high school in the area. As such, I have almost unlimited access to basketballs, climbing ropes, field hockey sticks, and pinnies (which are the mesh overshirts teams wear to distinguish themselves). I also have a key to the gymnasium. While I cannot give you any of this stuff, you are more than welcome to use it ON ANY WEEKEND YOU WANT!!! If you were to join a gym, this kind of service would cost you fifty or sixty dollars a month. I am offering it to you FOR NO CHARGE WHATSOEVER!!!

Also, in my wallet is an NEA discount and attractions card. This exclusive card is available only to National Education Association members, and gives you discounts at restaurants and area attractions. The card is yours. One small caveat: if you decide to use the card, you will probably have to pay my union dues first as I have fallen behind on my payments. But when you consider the money you will be saving, I'm pretty sure you'll agree it's well worth that small cost.

So that's the unlimited weekend use of the gym and sporting equipment, *and* the NEA discount and attractions card *and* the satisfaction of taking one for the team. Our team. The Doug and You team, which I am hereby naming "America's Team." And I'm going to get T-shirts made, too. For us to wear.

What do you say?

Erotic Fiction: The Mad Scientist

THERE. There in the moonlight she waits. Her dress rustles in the soft evening breeze; she is unspeakably gorgeous. She has a raccoon's tail, yes, but it is a gorgeous, fluffy raccoon's tail. Her damn father, the mad scientist, gave her this tail and you vow to one day avenge her.

"Monica," you say. You don't know why you say this—her name is Heather. She has been crying and doesn't seem to hear.

"Oh Steven," she whimpers. Her shoulders shake and a fresh torrent of tears pours from her eyes. "Steven, thank God you've come."

You take her in your arms. "I'm here now. What is it, my darling?"

"It's Papa," she says. "He's gone completely mad."

This is kind of a dumb thing for her to say. Her father was already mad. That's why everybody calls him "the mad scientist." They're not being ironic. He really is mad in both senses of the word: he's crazy, yes, but also very angry.

If his madness has become more pronounced, she might have said, "He's gone completely madder," but that doesn't sound right either, and you think it imprudent to correct her when she's sobbing.

"Somebody has to stop that man," you say. "And if the Department of Science won't do it, then I will."

"No!" she says, "He is too clever. Too strong. He has a team of henchmen, and they all have powerful animal tails."

"I don't care," you say, resolution creasing your otherwise flawless features. "He must be stopped."

"What will you do?" she asks, her face brightening for the first time as she lets out the tiniest fart.

"I will do what any man in my situation would do. I will call the IRS."

"The IRS?" she asks. Her face falls and you realize this is not the action she was hoping you'd take.

"Yes," you stammer. "To report that he doesn't pay taxes on the autographs he signs at those trade shows he attends." She looks despondent. I continue, "You're supposed to pay taxes on that. That's considered income!"

"Of course," she says, her tail drooping just a little in the moonlight. She turns away, toward the sea.

I don't know what else to say. I look at her, struggling to find the right words, the words that will make her love me again. But no words come.

"Go now, Steven," she says. "Just go."

"Monica," I say again, stupidly. Her name is not Monica. "Please."

It is over between us. Even after I call the IRS, even after they impose stiff fines on her father, even then she will not take me back.

The next time I see her, she has been given duck's feet and a piggy nose. And although I still care for her and feel terrible about my impotence in helping her, I am secretly relieved it is over between us because the raccoon tail I could handle, but a duck's feet and a piggy nose? Jesus. Now she just looks weird.

A Series of Letters to Celine Dion's Husband, René Angélil

Dear Mr. Angélil,

Greetings from the United States of America! How are things in Canada? I have never been there, but I am told Europe is beautiful.

A quick question before I begin: How do you pronounce your unusual last name? My hope is that it's pronounced "angelly," which I imagine would be the adverbial form of "angel." Wouldn't that be a beautifully descriptive word? Used in a sentence: "Celine Dion sang 'My Heart Will Go On' so angelly last night."

If that is not how you pronounce your name, do you think it is too late to start?

I have never written a fan letter before, but I felt compelled to drop you a note after seeing you on television alongside your wife, the incomparable Celine Dion. While she gets all the attention,

I am concerned that you do not receive the credit you deserve. If there is an overlooked, undervalued member of the Dion/Angélil team, I do not think it is Dion. She provides the angelly voice, yes, but you bring plenty to the table, too.

After all, there are undoubtedly lots of females out there who sing as well as your wife. China alone probably has a few million. Some of these women probably dance better, and I have no doubt that A LOT of these women look better (no offense).

So why is Celine a star, but they are not? I'll tell you exactly why: because even though China has millions of incredible China Ladies, it doesn't have a single René Angélil to discover them, guide them, manage them, and eventually, marry them.

This is why China will never be as powerful as Canada.

YOU were the one who discovered Celine when she was twelve. YOU were the one who mortgaged your house to raise money so she could record her first album. YOU did all this. She had the vision but YOU provided the eyeballs, without which vision is not possible.

Anyway, I just wanted to write and let you know that SOMEBODY out there appreciates you and thinks you are more than just a slightly creepy older guy who got lucky.

I am enclosing a self-addressed stamped envelope; if it's not too much trouble, can you please send an autograph?

> Your number one fan,
> Michael Ian Black

Dear Mr. Angélil,

While awaiting an autograph and response to my first letter, I thought of a couple more questions that I would like answered.

First, how do you keep your beard so neatly and evenly trimmed? I spent several hours today perusing photographs of you online, and in each one, your beard looks great. Personally, I do not have a beard. Part of the reason I don't is that I am concerned about keeping it tidy. Is there a particular brand of beard trimmer you recommend? Any advice you have in this regard would be greatly appreciated!

Equally important, I am interested in following in your footsteps as a talent scout and manager. Lately I have been hanging around my neighborhood middle school in the hopes of discovering my own Celine Dion. No luck yet. The only thing I've gotten for my trouble so far is a stern admonition from a VERY UPTIGHT school administrator. Apparently, even though my tax dollars help pay for that school, I am not welcome to take photographs of the students without permission.

Nobody said showbiz was easy, right, René?

You probably noticed I did not enclose a separate self-addressed stamped envelope this time. Feel free to use the one I already sent to respond to both letters.

> Your number one fan,
> Michael Ian Black

Dear René,

After sending my last letter, I was immediately seized with regret for not enclosing a separate self-addressed stamped envelope. What if the reason you have not yet responded is because you misplaced the first envelope I sent and have been waiting for me to send another? I would never forgive myself if we were unable to develop a correspondence (friendship?) for want of a lousy international stamp!!!

You will notice I am now enclosing TWO self-addressed stamped envelopes. That way you can either respond to my first two letters individually or together. (If you want to respond to this one as well, that's going to be on YOUR dime! (J/K! LOL!))

Until I hear back, I remain . . .

> Your fan,
> Michael Ian Black

Dear René,

What's the deal with your postal system? It has now been over two months since my initial letter to you, and I still have not heard back. I knew that your medical system was a cesspool, but I had never heard anything negative about your postal service. Forgive me for not knowing, but is Canada a third world country?

On the off chance that you have not received ANY of my previous letters, I am resending everything via FedEx. The only time I have ever had a problem with that company was the one time I attempted to send a package of smelling salts overseas.

(Because you are in the music biz, I think you know what I mean when I say "smelling salts." I mean cocaine.)

As you can see, I have also enclosed a return FedEx envelope for you. All of this letter writing and FedExing is starting to add up. If you want to throw a couple bucks into the envelope along with everything else, I wouldn't say no. (No Canadian money, please!!!)

Some good news on my end: I approached a young girl at the mall and asked if she wanted to become rich and famous. Guess what she said? YES!!!

I have already mortgaged my house, just like you, and I can't wait to get into the studio to start

"cutting" her first album. I'm thinking of calling it
The Next Celine Dion. What do you think?

Can I start planning a tour, or is this something I
need to discuss with her parents? Is there a legal way
to avoid telling them? How illegal is it if I don't?

Questions, questions, questions!!!

> Thanks,
> Michael Ian Black
> Talent Scout

René,

Trouble on the home front. Yesterday I received
a VERY ANGRY visit from Stacy's father. (Stacy is
the girl I wrote to you about a while ago.) Long
story short: despite my specific instructions NOT
to tell her parents about our project, she spilled
the beans. Half an hour later I'm dealing with an
irate man at my doorstep making all kinds of wild
accusations.

I explained to him the situation, told him all
about you, that you were behind this project, and
that if he had a problem with it, he should contact
you. He told me his lawyer (and possibly the police,
if you can believe it) would be in touch. Anyway,
don't be surprised if you get a call.

I think the whole thing is an effort to get a bigger piece of the merchandising. What do you think?

> Michael Ian Black
> Talent Scout
> Manager

René,

Once again, the FedEx guy passed my house without stopping. Once again I am forced to wonder if you are avoiding me. If so, I think I know why. You are jealous. You are jealous that I have found a future superstar (and bride?) while you are stuck playing second fiddle to the incomparable Celine Dion.

I don't blame you. My Stacy is younger, talent-eder, and so much less French Canadian than Celine Dion will ever be! And even though I have yet to hear her actually "sing," some talent doesn't need singing. Some talent just IS.

Also, I think it's only fair to let you know that my beard is now fully grown in. How does it look? Objectively speaking, incredible. Furthermore, it looks better than your beard. How much better? SOOOO much better. Don't believe me? I am enclosing a photo of myself as proof.

Yes, the photo is "in the buff," because I thought you should also see that I am in much better shape than you will ever be. Please notice that the sticker covering my privates is the kind that is easy to peel off and put back on. You will have to decide for yourself whether or not you can handle what's underneath.

Because of ongoing litigation involving my client's family, my lawyer has advised me that we no longer communicate. So be it. This will be my last letter. But before I sign off, I wanted to thank you, Mr. Angélil. You have given me so much more than your autograph. You gave me an education.

You taught me that dreams are more important than hard work and perseverance. You taught me that true talent will always overcome "the law." But mostly, you taught me that the music business is cruel and fickle and cruel. Yes, I said cruel twice because that is how cruel this business can be.

But I am not cruel, Mr. Angélil. I am a watcher of clouds and when I cast my eyes to the sky today, I see nothing but angelly days ahead.

> Sincerely,
> Michael Ian Black
> Talent Scout
> Manager
> Watcher of Clouds

Icky

"**ICKY**" is a word I would definitely use to describe myself. I do not see it listed here on this form. I see "Caucasian," "African-American," "Hispanic," "Native American," "Asian," and "Other," but no "Icky." I scan the list again. No. I use the blunted point of my number two pencil to fill in the oval marked "Other." Icky is closest to "Other," although the deep, secret racist part of me sometimes equates African-Americans with icky, too, but that is not my fault. It is the fault of my culture, which is inherently racist. I give fifty dollars a year to the United Negro College Fund as a way of absolving my own inherent white, racist, icky guilt. Yes, I am icky, and there is not a damn thing I can do about it.

Here's the deal with me: thirty years old, male, white (Caucasian), straight, perpetually single, out of shape, unemployed, irresponsible, bad-smelling, racist (previously mentioned), lazy, poorly groomed, and worth approximately $65 million.

None of my many friends knows about the money, but it's true. My net worth, in numerals, is 65,000,000.00, minus the fifty bucks I give to the United Negro College Fund each year. This is, I know, a lot of money. The kind of money that is so large it is literally inconceivable. Here's how I sometimes picture it when I am lying in my studio apartment trying to sleep: Imagine you walked into your house and found a $100 bill on the dresser. You would be pretty psyched. Anybody would be. A hundred dollars is a lot of money. Now imagine if you walked in and found ten $100 bills. That's a thousand dollars. A lot of fucking money, right? You're flipping out. You're calling people. "I just found a thousand bucks on my dresser!"

Okay, now imagine that once you find the thousand bucks, it occurs to you that there might be more money to find around. It seems unlikely, and there's no need to be greedy, but if there's an unexpected K lying around, who's to say there might not be more? So you look in your sock drawer, and there you find nine more bundles of ten $100 bills, bringing your total to ten thousand dollars. Now you're past the point of freaking out; now you're just scared. There's ten thousand dollars in $100 bills in and around your dresser. No more perky "Hey, guess what I just found!" telephone calls. No, you're not calling *anybody*. No, now your job is to rip the apartment down to the floorboards and see just how much money is hidden in this shitty Lower East Side studio apartment.

You decide to look under the mattress because that is historically where people conceal money. There, under the stained mattress you inherited when you took over the apartment, are nine more $10,000 stacks just like the one you have next to the bed. A hundred thousand dollars.

Now multiply that by a factor of ten. Already the image starts to get fuzzy, doesn't it? Up until ten thousand, it was easy. A hundred thousand, yes, you can kind of picture it when it's in neat $10,000 stacks. If the full mil is hard to fathom, just do it one at a time. Two $100,000 stacks. Now three. Up to ten. That's a million bucks. Multiply that by a factor of six. You've got six million dollars. Now consider this: that six million dollars represents less than 10 percent of what I am worth. It is to my worth what less than ten dollars is to a hundred—not very much.

That is one way I sometimes picture the amount of money in my control.

The sum is so vast that the only way I know how to deal with it is to totally ignore it. So that's what I do. I did nothing to earn the money, and do not feel right about claiming any of it. So I leave it alone and only occasionally turn it over in my mind when trying to fall asleep, the way some people count sheep or drink cough syrup.

The money is sitting in accounts at various international banks, all of it overseen by a buttoned-up family lawyer named Thatcher Emory Lloyd, who deals with all of the tax shit and investment shit and all the other shit that such a large amount of money generates. He's been the family lawyer for as long as I've been alive, and I imagine he will be around long after I am dead, because when you are as icky as I am, there can be no real hope for a long and fruitful life. There can be no hope really for anything, and even $65 million may not be enough to change that.

The form I am filling out at the moment is required by the New York State Department of Motor Vehicles to obtain a driver's license. I do not want a driver's license since I do not own a car and have no intention of purchasing a car, but I am finding it very difficult to accomplish certain tasks I want to accomplish without this form of identification.

For example, the other day I was attempting to secure a library card, which is something I do want, but was unable to get because I was unable to produce any identification other than a membership card to a video store, and I was almost unable to even get *that* without said identification, except that my best friend Jasmine works at the video store and vouched for my identity to her asshole manager, Keith, who, I swear to God, is thirteen years old. No exaggeration. He is thirteen motherfucking years old, and he runs that video store like it's his personal fiefdom, and if I wasn't so weak from chronic ickiness, I would put my fist right through that little fucker's face.

The library card, when I finally do get it, will be useful. Libraries are one of civilization's great gifts to itself. A place to go to read magazines and stare at college girls researching whatever it is college girls research, and maybe accidentally spill some coffee on one of them, and then apologize profusely while mopping off the girl's sweater and then, purely in the spirit of wanting to blot out the coffee before it stains, cop a feel.

Copping coffee feels off studious coeds half my age is a perfect example of a way in which I am icky. It is also the kind of behavior that can generate complaints from those same coeds. About two dozen complaints, in fact, which resulted in my being barred from my local library, which is another reason I am in the New York State Department of Motor Vehicles obtaining a driver's license with the name "Roland O. Wesbacher."

I am hoping that the name Roland O. Wesbacher, which is not my real name, will sound so different from Trevor P. Chellgren, which *is* my real name, that it will allow me to sneak back into the local library to resume my groping. If I am stopped at the door by an intrepid librarian who recognizes me despite the fake mustache I intend on donning, or the blonde wig with highlights, which I am already wearing, then I will simply produce this driver's license with the official seal of the great state of New York and say (in a carefully cultivated French accent), "Madam, you are mistaken. I am Roland O. Wesbacher."

And that should take care of that.

Looking around the waiting room here at the DMV, I am concerned that my blonde wig is already arousing suspicion among the more observant patrons. I have noticed more than one sniggering laugh aimed in my direction, and I am beginning to grow a touch paranoid. Of course, it is hard to say whether the pointing and laughter is due entirely to the wig or to my outfit, which is deliberately outlandish in order to deflect attention from my obviously fake hair. Now I fear that the plan might have backfired—the faux mink stole, feety pajamas, football shoulder pads, and blonde wig are actually creating *too much* attention.

Yes, people are definitely pointing and laughing, and I am realizing this entire operation is going down in flames before I have even approached Counter #2, which is where they take your picture and tell you to wait over by Counter #3. I should have known to abandon the project as soon as I got to Counter #1, where the woman told me if I thought I was going to get a driver's license looking like *that,* I had another think coming. Perhaps optimistically, I thought she was kidding, but now I am beginning to see she was not.

I cannot afford to be barred from another public institution. Sometimes discretion is the better part of valor, which is a fancy way of saying I need to get the hell out of here.

The thing to do now is to arrive at a plan of action that does not make me look foolish. My instinct is to just run out of the place, but that would give them the victory, and while I recognize that the battle here has been lost, the war is far from over, and even a small victory today may embolden them tomorrow. At the moment, I am a touch unclear as to who "they" are, but I know that I cannot give them an inch. I must escape this place unscathed.

A plan gradually forms. The first thing I do is fake a yawn. As I stretch, I nonchalantly unhook my shoulder pads and let them slide to the carpeted floor, as if to say, "Okay, football shoulder pads, you've done your work for the day. Take a load off, guys."

Then I pretend I have something in my eye. (For the sake of my inner monologue, it is sand grit picked up while surfing in Maui.) I make a good show of pain for everybody at the DMV, grimacing and pointing at my eye. I nudge the woman next to me, who is about sixty and Cambodian or something, and who does not seem to speak much English, and say, "I have some sand in my eye." She looks a little scared and nods, but I wasn't really speaking to her. I was talking to the security guard, who I know is watching my every move.

And this is where the plan gets, I must admit, brilliant. Rather than flee the scene, rather than scurry away like a scared little squirrel, I make straight for the enemy. Right hand pressed to eye, left hand dragging football shoulder pads, I walk up to the guard and say, "Excuse me, is there a water fountain in here? I need to rinse out my eye because of the sand I got in it when I was surfing in Maui." The guard shifts his body weight, and I know I have him exactly where I want him—totally flummoxed.

I can just hear his feeble thoughts tumbling around in that pea brain of his: *Maybe this is how they dress in Maui.* What a stooge. He stares at me for a couple seconds, and I stare right back. Two gladiators fighting to the death in ancient Greece, or Rome, or wherever ancient gladiators fought to the death. After an eternity, he jerks his thumb toward the restrooms and says, "Over there."

Trying not to smirk, I thank the man and proceed to walk in *exactly the opposite direction*, right out the door. That should have him scratching his head for the better part of the rest of his life.

How strange, I think, as I leave the DMV. *Here I am, a well-liked and attractive man worth $65 million, unable to procure a practically free tiny plastic card that will allow me to use an entirely free public service for the purpose of bettering myself through literature and also copping feels from college girls. What a strange, paradoxical country this is.* At that moment, I feel disappointed, yes, but oddly patriotic. I may be icky, but my country is good.

I deposit the football shoulder pads that I am still dragging behind me in a trash pile along the sidewalk. *These shoulder pads have served me well,* I think, as I lay them on top of several smelly trash bags that, if I had to guess, contain more than a little used kitty litter. *Yes, they have served me well, and they deserve a hero's burial.* I compose a little eulogy to the shoulder pads along the lines of "We are gathered today to celebrate these shoulder pads, which protected countless young men in battle on the gridiron and one young man in the battlefield of the motor vehicle department. They did their duty honorably and with valor." Then I hum "Taps" and snap into a smart salute. Several blocks away, a truck backfires. Above, the sky has turned a majestic crimson, and just as I finish the final bars of the song, a flock of pigeons shoots overhead in formation, and I have to choke down tears as I pivot on one heel and step away.

A Few Words About My Jug Band

FOR the last few years I've been playing washboard in a local jug band, the Salt Cracker Crazies. Mostly we play country fairs, rodeos, jug band–themed birthday parties, jug band–themed funerals, that sort of thing. Our biggest gig was probably when we played 50 Cent's record-release party for his last album. You wouldn't think that 50 Cent would be into jug bands, and you'd be right. He wasn't. Curtis didn't enjoy our music *at all*, although later in the night he graciously told me he thought my washboard strumming was "bumpin'."

People often approach me after one of our gigs wanting to know how I got into playing the washboard. I was an all-state defensive back in high school and played college ball for Auburn. During my junior year, I blew out my knee, which ended any thoughts I had about entering the NFL. But the injury allowed me to focus on other things, like writing my radical feminist poetry. It also gave me plenty of time to explore the campus. Of course I was on crutches, so I couldn't wander far, but one night, with exams behind me and football out of the picture, I found myself hobbling into a basement coffee shop. What I saw there changed my life.

It was around ten o'clock on a Monday night. The place

was mostly empty, but on a tiny stage in the back was a band. A jug band. I'd heard of jug bands before, of course, but I thought they went extinct with the dinosaurs (although I didn't think the two events were necessarily related). Well, if jug bands no longer existed, these guys never got the memo! They were hootin' and hollerin' and playing a wild skiffle, although I didn't know the word "skiffle" back then. I just knew the sound was infectious and completely unlike the usual music I listened to (Iron Maiden, Slayer, Natalie Merchant, etc.). This was organic music, music that sounded like what compost would taste like if you ate compost and didn't throw up. It was a wild concoction of bluegrass, jazz, and country twang all thrown together into a musical potluck supper upon which I feasted. With my ears. I ear-feasted.

At the center of this melodious scrum was a wild-eyed, long-haired desperado whose name I later found out was Mitch "the Snitch" Greenburg. Mitch was playing the washboard, that humble, anachronistic laundry implement. He was really going at it, too, smacking and shaking and coaxing beautiful music from that thing. Watching Snitch that night, I knew what I wanted to do with the rest of my life. Comedy. But I also knew that I would like to learn the washboard. So I approached him after the show and inquired about lessons.

Mitch just looked at me and laughed. "You can't learn the washboard, boy," he said. I found it strange that he was calling me "boy," because he was only nine years old. "It's just sumpin' you feel." I wanted to know more, but his mom told me Mitch had to get to bed because it was a school night, and she led him away into the misty Alabama night.

The band was called the Sweet and Sour Catfish Variety Jug Band, and they were all local Alabamans. Their leader was a man who called himself Jessup Lowe. He alternately described himself as a minstrel, an employee of the city parks and rec department, and a werewolf. Personally, I think he was all three. Not literally, of course. I don't think he *really* worked for the parks and rec department.

Jessup lived in a little house on the edge of town with his wife, a mountainous woman named Lilybeth. She played wash bucket bass with the Fish, and she was the only one who could control Jessup's temper. Jessup got angry when he drank, and he drank a lot. When he got sauced and said something maybe he shouldn't have, Lilybeth had no problem cocking back her arm and punching him right in the face. That usually shut him up, but not always, and they used to have some terrible brawls. Nowadays, we call that sort of thing a "dysfunctional relationship," but back then we just called it love.

Jessup and Lilybeth were the heart and soul of that happy little jug band. There were others, of course, in the group: Snitch on washboard, "Wee" Willie Gladstone on harmonica, Jake "'n Bake" Stickman on fiddle, and Jo "Damn It" Nabbit on the horn. It was a queer group. They never hung out together except for rehearsals and shows. But when they played, they *played*. Over time, I got to know them all, and Jessup and Lilybeth even offered to let me stay with them the summer after my junior year when I was working on a road crew to make some money. I took them up on it, but moved out the night of the first full moon after Jessup tried to eat my face.

One day I was hanging out with the band before a gig when they got a call. Mitch had the chicken pox and wouldn't be able to make it to the show. A jug band without a washboard? That's like a discotheque without any transvestites: it can still exist, yes, but what's the point?

The Fish held a quick meeting. Did I want to sit in? Jake 'n Bake had a spare washboard with him—it was mine for the taking.

"But I don't know how to play," I almost blurted out. But then I remembered what Mitch had said to me all those months before. "It's just sumpin' you feel."

"Give me that thing," I said, grabbing it from Jake's hand. Later, Jake told me I grabbed it too hard, pulling one of his tendons, but at the time he was taken with my enthusiasm and he didn't want to make me feel bad.

I'll never forget that night. It was a big crowd for the group—fifteen—and at least half of them were specifically there to see the band. The rest came for the foosball. But that was fine with us. Jessup always had a theory about the audience. They might be there for the foosball or the $2 pitchers or the wet T-shirt contest, but by the end of the night, they were staying for the Sweet and Sour Catfish Variety Jug Band. His theory was wrong, of course; if they stayed it was mostly because they were alcoholics. But the theory made Jessup feel better, so nobody ever contradicted him.

When we lit into our first skiffle, I felt as though I'd been playing the washboard all my life. I stomped and slithered and shook that thing within an inch of its life. Lilybeth told me I was a natural, which made me feel great. Then she told me that I was most likely a Crystal Child from another dimension, which made me feel confused. I decided to take the first statement and disregard the second, leaving me feeling great.

Mitch Greenburg recovered from the pox a short time later and rejoined the band. Shortly after that, I dropped out of Auburn and rode the boxcars for a while with my bindle and my washboard, making music on the rails and in pickup jug bands wherever the trains stopped.

And then something happened, something called life. Somewhere along the way, I put down my washboard. Got married. Had a couple kids. Bought a house and a couple of Maseratis, helped deliver a baby calf. And one day the skiffle just went out of me. Until, that is, I found myself alone sipping a margarita at a local Mexican joint a couple of years ago. The strolling mariachi trio had just finished their umpteenth rendition of "La Cucaracha" and were packing away their things when I heard a familiar scrittle-scratch coming from behind me. I looked and there was a wild-eyed, long-haired guy, probably twenty-five years old with a kazoo in his mouth and a washboard on his lap. Even under all that clown makeup, I knew I was looking at Mitch Greenburg. He was a washboard-strumming birthday clown and the kids at the party were rapt. I watched Mitch tie some balloon animals, play "Knick Knack Paddy Whack" on the spoons, trip over his big clown shoes, and, of course, strum that beat-up old washboard. Same old Snitch. The kids loved him. So did I.

I thought about going up to him after the party but decided against it. Instead, I watched him pack his washboard into his polka-dot pickup truck and drive off into the misty Connecticut night. He left that Mexican joint alone, but nobody who plays the washboard so sweet could ever truly be alone.

As I watched him go, I resolved right then and there that I was going to have my own jug band. The next day I took an ad out in the *Pennysaver*. "Wanted," I wrote, "Scalawags and Broom Jumpers for an Old-Fashioned Good Time Jug Band."

Soon the Salt Cracker Crazies were born. If you ever want to hear some down-home jug band tunes, give us a call. We're not the greatest musicians in the world, but we've got a lot of heart and a lot of nicknames. Besides, jug band music isn't something you hear—it's something you feel. With your ears. You ear-feel it. Which, I guess technically, is the same thing as hearing.

Chapter 19 of My Science Fiction Epic, *The Pirates of Dagganon 6*, Which I Am Only Able to Write Because of a Generous Grant from the Makers of Barq's Root Beer

CHAPTER 19

Sassalak!

Tridor slammed the qibec crystals into overdrive, but they had no effect. The propulsion force was simply too strong. Ahead, the dark planet pulled them toward it, and there was nothing they could do.

"Divert all power to main thrusters," Tridor yelled.

"She won't hold together!" barked Aga, her skin changing from a mottled green to a fiery crimson. She was even more beautiful red.

Tridor pushed the chameleoform's beauty from his mind and responded, "Either we punch this baby out of here now or we end up in the clutches of Starforce Security. And I don't think any of us wants that."

Aga nodded and sprinted from the command deck. He spoke into the com. "Twi-Twi, where are you?"

The naraboo's familiar chirp came back at him almost instantly. The little guy was probably trying to figure out how to wring more power from the pneumatic crystal drive. One good thing about naraboos: they were tiny, but they sure were feisty.

Tridor opened up a cold Barq's root beer and contemplated his options. None of them were good. Maybe they could escape the planet's gravitational field, but then what? The qibec crystals would be depleted, leaving the pirate ship drifting hopelessly through the quadrant. Or they could allow themselves to descend to the Sassalak surface. But then what? Starforce Security would be tracking them. The moment the ship touched land, they'd throw him and his crew into a laser cell. Once in, it was unlikely any of them would ever get out. There had to be another way. But what was it? Tridor took another sip from his Barq's. The drink's sharp effervescence gave him an idea.

"Aga, Twi-Twi—get your pirate butts up here now!"

The words were hardly out of his mouth before the chameleoform and naraboo were at his side. Twi-Twi whistled and chirruped in his peculiar patois: What were they going to do? Aga looked on with interest. Her red skin had faded to a grayish pink. He understood the mood underneath the hue—like the rest of the crew, she was tense and anxious.

"I was drinking this Barq's root beer when I had a thought—"

"Those are delicious," whistled Twi-Twi.

"Quiet, damn it!" Twi-Twi's furry face fell. Ordinarily, Tridor hated to yell at his little friend, but they were running out of time.

"Sorry, boss," he chirped.

Tridor grunted, and pointed to the frothy glass of root beer. "Look at how these bubbles float to the surface." Aga and Twi-Twi crowded around the glass. It was true. Hundreds of bubbles floated up from the bottom. The carbonation produced air bubbles that were lighter than the surrounding liquid. The bubbles not only helped give Barq's its bite but also provided a possible way out of the trio's predicament. Tridor explained his idea, watching as Aga's shade turned from pink to a confused gray to an excited canary yellow. She understood!

The pirates ran (and in Twi-Twi's case, flew) toward the airlock. They would only have one chance at this. Already, the ship was beginning to jostle as it hit Sassalak's thick atmosphere. Only minutes ago, Tridor was cursing his luck at emerging from hyperspace into the Sassalak system, but now he thought maybe it had been a blessing in disguise. The three space pirates fastened themselves into their oxygen exchange suits and waited for Tridor's signal.

Outside, methane swirled around the ship in roiling clouds. If Starforce Security didn't know they were there yet, they would soon.

"Unidentified cruiser, identify yourself!" There they were. Right on cue. The transmission was partially garbled. Tridor tried to buy some time.

"Repeat. Repeat, please." Tridor signaled to his compatriots to stand by. Aga began turning an impatient purple. A couple more seconds was all they needed. Just enough time to break through the thickest part of the atmosphere.

"Unidentified cruiser, this is Starforce Security. If you do not identify yourself immediately, you will be intercepted and boarded."

How would he explain a ship filled to bursting with powdered carjamin seeds, the most valuable plant in the galaxy? Answer—he couldn't.

"Uh, yes, Starforce Security. We are the *Gamma Pole* agri-ship from the United States of Earth," Tridor improvised as his finger hovered over the dump button. "We're carrying a load of hydropods. Our paperwork should be in order."

Twi-Twi whistled as the sky began to lighten. Any second now.

"We don't have any records of a *Gamma Pole.* Please hover and prepare to be boarded."

"Board THIS!" screamed Tridor, flipping off the transmitter and swigging down the rest of his icy cold Barq's; the last swig was as good as the first. "NOW!" he yelled to his fellow pirates.

Four hands and twelve naraboo fingers began feverishly dumping the ship's nitrogen and hydrogen. The dense air outside began lifting the ship. They had become like one of those carbonated bubbles; the ship rose, accelerating as it went.

"It's working!" yelled Aga.

"Not yet it's not," muttered Tridor. Soon they were in the methane exosphere. This was the crucial part of the plan. If he'd calculated correctly, the thick methane would react with the nitrogen blowing from their ship, causing the ship to rocket from the planet as if it were a carbonation bubble in a shaken bottle of scintillating Barq's root beer.

"Hang on!" Tridor screamed, although the warning was unnecessary. Aga was strapped to her chair, her skin blending in with the fabric. Twi-Twi was strapped to Tridor, his tiny fingers grasping Tridor's pant leg. The ship began rumbling, quaking. Either they were going to be ejected from the planet's atmosphere or the superstructure would crumble from the stress.

A red warning light blinked on the control board. The qibec crystals were overheating! If it didn't happen soon, it never would. Tridor could see the ship's hull contracting and buckling around him.

Suddenly, they heard a loud BANG! The ship was speeding up, accelerating past its tolerance threshold. Aga screamed. Tridor caught Twi-Twi's eyes. They were round but unexpressive. *Brave little naraboo*, he thought as he felt his body pushed to the floor. *We're not going to make it*, he thought. The ship wouldn't hold, and it was all his fault.

And then, just like that, they were free. Far behind was Sassalak. They were back in the Ungoverned Territories.

Slowly the three space pirates picked themselves up from the floor, inspecting themselves and one another for injuries. There were none.

"We did it," said Tridor.

"You did it," said Aga, turning an expressive green. He'd never seen that color on her before, but he knew exactly what it meant. "Excuse us, Twi-Twi," said Aga, moving toward the man who only days before had been her sworn enemy.

Twi-Twi fluttered from the room.

Tridor, the confident ship's captain, suddenly found himself at a loss for words. His throat felt dry as the chameleoform approached. "Barq's?" he asked, holding up a can of the refreshing soft drink that had saved their lives that day, as it had so many times before.

"Maybe later," she said, kissing him. "You're going to need it."

My Top 50 New Year's Resolutions

1. Quit smoking. This one is easy because I don't smoke.
2. Lose weight. Also easy because I am anorexic.
3. Kill at least one large animal. Kind of a weird resolution, I know, but I figure killing a large animal (like an elk or a moose) is something every man should do at least once. I'm going to do it this year. The twist? I'm going to use anthrax.
4. Get the tires rotated on my car. Self-explanatory and, again, easy.
5. Make interstellar travel a reality. This one is a little more ambitious considering my limited skills set (see my essay on page 87: "When I Finally Get Around to Building My Robot, This Is What It Will Be Like"), but somebody's got to do it, and it might as well be me. It seems like the key is figuring out how to get around the fact that nothing can travel faster than the speed of light. Once I do that, the rest should be a piece of cake.
6. Stop referring to my wife as "my little homunculus."
7. Fewer rampages.
8. Give Katie Couric a shot on the *CBS Evening News*. She's been struggling in the ratings, and I certainly haven't been

doing my part to help. Besides, it's very hard to jerk off to Charles Gibson.

9. Use more Axe body spray.

10. Go deep undercover. Even if it's not for any particular purpose. Just infiltrate some organization. Any organization at all.

11. Learn typesetting and harmonica.

12. Take more photographs of morbidly obese people at water parks.

13. Witness a murder.

14. Start collecting ivory. So beautiful and increasingly hard to collect; prices will undoubtedly skyrocket if elephants become extinct. Kill elephants, which would also take care of resolution #3.

15. Write a highly successful, fictionalized memoir of my drug abuse and subsequent jail time.

16. Do everything in my power to destroy Tom Hanks.

17. Finally invent "ice cream burrito." I've been talking about this for years and haven't done anything about it. One day somebody's going to get there first and I'm going to be kicking myself.

18. Either develop scoliosis or quit talking about developing scoliosis. As far as scoliosis goes, this year is definitely "shit or get off the pot" time.

19. Give panhandling a *real* chance.

20. Commit grand larceny. What am I going to steal? That's easy. A backhoe.

21. Apply for every credit card that comes in the mail. Ideally, I will end up with a different credit card for every day of

the year. Once I have them all, I will withdraw the maximum cash advance I can on every single one and then fake my own death.

22. Ferret out J. D. Salinger in order to tell him that I think *The Catcher in the Rye* is a really good book.

23. More cornholing.

24. Compile definitive list of "Best American Fudge Shops." Sell list for a hundred dollars a pop. Sit back and watch the money roll in.

25. Learn the lesson that playing grabby ass isn't fun for waitresses.

26. Get trademark on word "crantastic," used to describe a particularly delicious cranberry.

27. Figure out a way to get legit handicap plates without becoming legitimately handicapped.

28. Give strangers more advice about how to raise their children. While I do not claim to be an expert in raising children, I do have some pretty strong opinions on the subject, developed over years of doing things exactly right.

29. Stop relying on my salt lick to get my daily allowance of salt. It grosses people out and there are definitely better ways to get my iodine.

30. Quit showboating. It only pisses people off, especially when it's over stupid stuff (like being the tallest person in the library, etc.).

31. Don't call in bomb threats to get out of dental appointments. This is, without a doubt, one of my worst habits.

32. Stop saying "zygote" when I mean "fetus."

33. Sell some military secrets to the Chinese. This one's going

to be tough as I do not have access to any military secrets, and I don't know any Chinese people. But on the plus side, I recently saw *Patton*.

34. Try harder to remember that tomatoes aren't the enemy.

35. Remake my wardrobe to be more "fashion forward." That means more scuba flippers, light-up bow ties, and oversize hockey jerseys and less Boba Fett costumes, wax lips, and compression hose.

36. If I'm going to burn rubber tires, I need to do it when the wind is blowing *away* from the nursing home next door.

37. Stop making jokes in the security line at the airport. There's no need to impress the TSA guys so that they'll come away from our encounters thinking, *That guy is hilarious.*

38. Don't use charitable giving as a way to feel smug. This one's going to be hard for me because charitable giving is one of my primary ways of feeling smug, both toward the people to whom I am donating and toward the people who did not give. It's two-for-one smugness and it has to stop.

39. Clean out my high school locker. It's been almost twenty years, and I imagine things are getting a little rank in there.

40. Cut down on my carbon footprint by making everybody come to me instead of the other way around. Let the dead Earth be on *their* consciences for once.

41. Learn and use cool handshakes.

42. Learn and use my children's names.

43. Pitch my idea for the television show *World's Strongest Rock Star*. When an executive asks, "Will anybody care how far Hootie can shot-put?" answer, "Yes."

44. Give serious consideration to adopting a baby, but don't.

45. Quit disparaging wallpaper. There's a lot of great wallpaper out there and when I make generalizations about "all wallpaper," it makes me look ignorant. I'm better than that.

46. Give up the pseudonym I use when writing my radical feminist poetry. At a certain point, I have to trust that my comedy audience will embrace my radical feminist poetry and my radical feminist poetry audience will embrace my comedy. The two do not have to be mutually exclusive.

47. Write more thank-you cards, but draw fewer swastikas on them.

48. Develop a taste for fine port, talk about it a lot, and then snicker when people are ignorant about the drink. Could be a good replacement for feeling smug (see resolution #38).

49. Taste and rank every Jelly Belly flavor according to how much it tastes like what it is supposed to taste like. Compile results into a definitive list. Sell each copy for a hundred dollars. Sit back and watch the money roll in.

50. Put up that birdhouse.

Hey, Doritos, Get Your Shit Together

THERE was a time when Doritos made one product—Nacho Cheese Doritos. This was a revolutionary chip. Even its shape was revolutionary. A triangle-shaped chip? Yes. Oh, fuck yes. Nacho Cheese flavored? Hell to the fuck yes. They came out in 1966. Nobody else was mass-marketing tortilla chips back then, let alone flavoring the shit out of them. Doritos was the Google of its time, so far superior to any other chip out there that to put it in the same snack food category as, say, Lay's Potato Chips would be an insult to the term "snack food category."

Then they upped their game. When I was seven or eight, Doritos took it to the next level. How? By creating the "Taco Flavored Dorito." How much did the Taco Dorito taste like an actual taco? Zero. It tasted zero much like a regular taco. Instead, it tasted better. Somehow Doritos managed to perfect the perfect food. If you've read this far in the book, you are no doubt already aware of my fondness for all things taco-related. And yet somehow the good people—nay, great people—at Doritos managed to create a taste so distinctive, so marvelous, it trumped even tacos' inherent wonderfulbility. And in doing so, they even managed to somehow make me dislike Mexicans less.

The Taco Dorito was spicier than the original Nacho Cheese Dorito, and miraculously seemed to contain more sodium than a chip that size should be able to handle. In chemistry, I remember learning about saturation and supersaturation. Somehow, perhaps using advanced twenty-fifth-century magical powers of nanotechnology they acquired from a downed UFO, the Doritos people supersaturated the Taco Dorito with deliciousness. That is to say they put so much deliciousness in that product, it threatened the very stability of matter itself. How did they do it? I don't know and, frankly, I don't want to know. Even the Keebler elves never had that kind of power.

It was the perfect chip.

And then it disappeared. The Taco Dorito entered the Bermuda Triangle of snack foods. One minute it was there, the next gone without a word to anybody. It vanished without so much as a "fare-thee-well." And nobody besides me was even talking about it. Why was I the only one who seemed to notice or care? Several years later, when they canceled that stupid Claire Danes show, thousands of people wrote letters to the network demanding it be brought back, and you couldn't even eat that show. Nobody did that for the Taco Dorito. Nobody did a goddamned thing.

At first I thought maybe Doritos was playing mind games with us. Or maybe they were copying the folks at Mallomars, who release their splendid cookie only once a year. But as the years went by, I realized that unless they were implementing a "Taco Doritos only come out once in seven years like the cicada" marketing strategy, chances were Taco Doritos were gone for good.

Why?

Having been associated with almost exclusively failed projects over the course of my career, I would like to hazard a guess. My gut tells me the rest of America wasn't nearly as wild about Taco Doritos as this lonely New Jersey boy. My guess is that Americans preferred the safe, predictable, even (I will say it because nobody else has the courage) *boring* flavor of the Nacho Cheese Dorito. Maybe the rest of the nation felt the Taco Dorito was too spicy, too ethnic, too *different*. And maybe, I suspect, they feel the same way about me.

From that point on, Doritos lost their luster in my eyes. They really started to slide downhill after the Cool Ranch Dorito was introduced. First of all, I don't like the idea of Doritos in a blue bag. Doritos and blue clash. That's why in all of professional sports there is not a single team with orange and blue uniforms except the Denver Broncos who have never won anything (except several Super Bowls). Will I eat a Cool Ranch Dorito? Sure, because despite everything I still enjoy Doritos. I love their wholesome crunch, I love the flavor granules that scrape off the chip and wedge themselves into the whorls of my fingertips, allowing me the orgasmic pleasure of scraping off the taste with my teeth when I am done with my chips. To me, that's like a Doritos dessert. But I don't love them as much as I once did, back when the Taco Dorito was around.

Since then, Doritos has introduced a plethora of flavor choices, all of which are now preceded by an unnecessary adjective. "Sizzlin' Picante," for example. Or "Smokin' Cheddar

BBQ." Setting aside the fact that I don't want to eat any chip that combines the tastes of cheddar cheese and smoke, I don't know why the marketing folks at Doritos feel the need to add descriptive modifiers to their chip names. Nor do I know why they feel the need to drop the g's at the ends of "sizzling" and "smoking."

Actually, I do know.

Recently I did some work for the people at PepsiCo, under the aegis of the Sierra Mist banner. What you may not know is that Frito-Lay, the makers of Doritos, is owned by PepsiCo. A couple of years ago Pepsi invited me to go to the Super Bowl, which they sponsor. As part of the weekend's festivities, they had a big breakfast/marketing meeting/ cult worship ceremony in which all of the different PepsiCo brands showed off their upcoming commercials. When it was Doritos' turn to go, an exuberant, amped-up dude bounded onto the stage and began describing the Doritos brand. He used words like youthful and fun-loving. But one word really stuck with me that day. "Doritos are outrageous," he said.

Outrageous?

I wasn't sure what he meant. Did he mean that the chip itself is outrageous? Or did he mean that outrageous people, as some part of their outrageousness, enjoyed Doritos? Or was it that Doritos forced ordinary people to do outrageous things? And what kind of outrageous act would be acceptable to PepsiCo? For example, I imagine killing a hooker would probably not be okay. What if the killer employed the "Doritos made me do it" defense? I'm not an expert on such matters, but it seems to me that could be very bad press for the entire PepsiCo family.

I think, to the corporate lackeys who make beverages and snack foods, dropping the *g* off the end of words = outrageous. The thought perhaps being that some square English teacher will see the bags on the shelves and say out loud, "They dropped the *g*. That's outrageous!" As he stews in his indignation, a moptopped skater kid will whiz by, grabbing the Doritos bag so quickly that the resultant breeze will blow off the professor's toupee. That's outrageous!!!

Maybe Doritos marketers think that people who routinely drop their *g*'s are rule breakers, and a chip that does the same will appeal to such people. But this is a slippery slope. That same skater kid (who is already breaking the rules by skateboarding in the supermarket) might decide that Doritos are awesome, but he doesn't want to pay for them. So he just skates past the outraged cashiers and out the door, thus giving the proverbial middle finger to all of society.

OUTRAGEOUS!!!

PepsiCo, I suspect, doesn't want any actual outrageousness of this sort going on. Instead, they want the idea of outrageousness safely contained in a plastic snack bag. They want us to express our outrageousness through the radical, subversive act of eating a corn chip. Consider their marketing campaign that year. Regular people were encouraged to create their own commercial for Doritos. The winning entry would be shown during the Super Bowl. OUTRAGEOUS!!! Somebody needs to explain to me how the act of creating a thirty-second television commercial for a multinational food and beverage conglomerate could be perceived as anything other than utterly bourgeois, which is a French word meaning "fucking stupid." The only thing outrageous about it was that they weren't getting paid.

Then there is the issue of some of the newer additions to the Doritos family, like the 100-calorie Mini Bites Doritos. These are bags of Doritos carefully apportioned so that if one eats the whole bag, that person will be ingesting exactly one hundred calories of outrageousness. You can't have it both ways, Doritos. You can't be crazy and impulsive and also a 100-calorie minibag. Or what about the Reduced Fat Nacho Cheese and Cool Ranch Doritos? Reduced fat? OUT-RAGEOUS!

Go to the Doritos website. There you will find all kinds of outrageousness: electric guitars, speedboats, seaplanes, plus advertisements for other products like the Xbox and MTV. Why does a website for one product advertise other products? That's easy: outrageous corporate synergy. MTV? Outrageous. Xbox? Outrageous. There's also an interactive video game called "The Quest," whose tagline is "Guessing the flavor is just the beginning." Honestly, I don't ever want to be in a situation where I am "guessing the flavor."

The scenario I want to avoid is as follows:

Person 1: "Here. Eat this."

Me: "What is it?"

Person 1: "Guess!"

Anytime guessing the flavor is the beginning, I'm fairly confident I know the ending: diarrhea. But maybe I'm just not outrageous enough to play a video game on a website for corn chips.

Why can't we just have chips? Why do we need slogans and branding and treasure? I just want to be able to eat my salt and trans fats in peace. And I want those trans fats to be taco flavored, just like they used to be. Either I'm just not getting the world anymore or else the world is just gettin' more outrageous.

I Just Bought a Shitload of Fireworks

HAPPY Fourth of July, everybody. Tomorrow is the day our nation celebrates our independence by eating grilled meat and blowing stuff up. Boy, am I excited. I just bought a shitload of fireworks and I cannot wait to set them off. Yes, I got firecrackers and cherry bombs. Yes, I got M-80s. Yes, I got dazzlers and whippers and German Schnauzers. I also got some yip daddies, cocobongos, and flashbang wiggle worms. And because I am such a loyal customer to the particular fireworks emporium where I made my purchases, I also got some fireworks that aren't available yet to the general public. These are "beta fireworks," which I have agreed to test out before they hit the market. I will describe some of them for you now:

- Griddle Poppers. This small explosive device launches several McDonald's McGriddles fifty feet into the air. Just as they reach their apex, they explode, leaving a phosphorescent trail of maple syrup lighting up the night sky. Beautiful.

- Whizzing Octosnatches. These are eight, tiny, whizzing vaginas that are sent screaming upward at nearly the speed of sound. When they blow up, they spell out the word "Christmas." I'm not sure why.

- Regis Philbin's Head. This is exactly as it is described. A papier-mâché bust of the popular morning-talk-show host. When the lit fuse reaches the base, the top of Regis's head blows off, unleashing a flurry of multicolored flaming paper butterflies that flutter around for a few moments before falling, charred, back to earth. Truly magnificent.

- Old PC. This highly explosive device is basically a quarter stick of TNT housed inside an old PC. Stand back from this one because when it goes off, shards of plastic can easily get into your eyes. Fun, but not recommended for kids.

- Space Shuttle *Challenger* Explosion. Again, just as advertised. You light the fuse on this baby, stand back, and watch it take off to the heavens. Then, about ninety seconds after liftoff, it blows up. Not amusing at all. Apparently, they're also working on a *Columbia* model, which breaks up on reentry. I would probably not purchase either of these.

- Land Mines. These are smaller versions of real land mines employed by the military. They are nonlethal, but if you step on one, they provide quite a shock and a pretty painful burn. Definitely fun and thrilling, but if you decide to bury them in your backyard before your picnic, make sure your guests are wearing flip-flops.

- Michael Vick Brand Hanging Pit Bull Explod-o-Piñata. Despite the awkward name, this one is actually very colorful and fun. Basically it's designed to look like a pit bull that just lost a dog fight. The idea is, you hang it from a tree, then light the thing on fire. It sparks for several minutes, then eventually "dies." Very bright and colorful. Question: Does Michael Vick receive any money from this? I hope not, because that would be wrong.

- Bucket of Whirling Gravy. The title pretty much says it all. It's a little bit like the Griddle Poppers, but instead of flying into the sky, the bucket just stays on the ground and, when lit, sprays steaming hot gravy over everything in a fifty-foot radius. Keep away from the house and do not use near bears.

- The UNICEF Box of Coins. This is a classic case of "good idea gone bad." Basically, this firework replicates the classic UNICEF box that children take from house to house, asking for spare change to donate to the world's needy children. You light the thing, stand back, and watch it explode. That's all fine and good, but they filled it with real coins, which then come raining down on you from the sky, which is terrifying and extremely dangerous.

- Frogs. These are not fireworks. They are just frogs, and I wonder if the guy put them in my bag as a joke.

Have a great holiday, everyone. Eat a lot, go swimming, and think about our Founding Fathers, who not only created the greatest country in the world, but did so while wearing knickers and wigs.

In Conclusion: A First Draft of the Acceptance Speech I Plan to Give Upon Receiving Some Kind of Important Literary Prize for Writing This Book

Greetings ~~losers~~ fellow writers,

When I first sat down to write *My Custom Van,* I ~~totally knew~~ had no idea the profound effect it would have—not just on ~~stoners~~ young people, but on society as a whole. How could I know essays such as "This Is How I Party" and "Why I Used a Day-Glo Magic Marker to Color My Dick Yellow" would strike such a resonant chord with so many? Answer: ~~focus groups~~ I couldn't.

Throughout those ~~leisurely, booze-filled afternoons~~ torturous days when I was ~~playing Tetris~~ struggling to put pen to paper, I sometimes wondered if I would ever complete this anthology. Perhaps I was being too hard on myself; analyzing the text, I insisted that each word be ~~written~~ perfect. The effort almost killed me!!!!!!!!

(NOTE: Possibly insert joke about how the food at the awards dinner almost killed me, too.)

But then I ~~Googled~~ stumbled across a speech that ~~I didn't~~

~~understand~~ changed my perception of what it means to be a writer.

Upon accepting his Nobel Prize for Literature in 1962, John Steinbeck, who I am told wrote some excellent books, said the following:

> The ancient commission of the writer has not changed.
> He is charged with exposing our many grievous faults
> and failures, with dredging up to the light our dark and
> dangerous dreams for the purpose of improvement.

How right that guy was, ~~losers~~ friends. How right he was. ~~To repeat: how truly right he was.~~

When I discovered Steinbeck's words, I realized that I was doing the same exact thing as him ~~only better~~. I too was using man's "grievous faults and failures" to illuminate his "dark and dangerous dreams" (See: "How to Approach the Sensitive Question: Anal?" page 169). Steinbeck and I are like ~~two kittens playing with the same ball of yarn~~ kindred spirits. How wonderful to discover that my dream of improving mankind was shared by none other than one of ~~England's~~ America's greatest ~~Elizabethan~~ modern writers.

For all my ~~missed deadlines~~ difficulties, however, this book was a joy for me to write. But more importantly, it was a joy for you to read. You love this book. How do I know? Because you're giving me this cool literary prize.

When I first received the news that I had won, I wondered aloud, "~~Who did my publisher have to blow to make this happen?~~ "Am I truly worthy of such an honor?" ~~Hell to the yeah!~~

Humility prevents me from answering in the affirmative; I only hope to prove myself worthy of this esteemed award.

Of course, a prize such as this also carries with it a responsibility to use my newfound notoriety for the public good. As such, I have decided to dedicate myself to ~~stopping the war in Iraq~~ raising autism awareness ~~overthrowing the government~~ ~~making horsemeat "the other red meat"~~ ~~teaching Chinese kids to bowl~~ ~~figuring out a way to befriend Leonardo DiCaprio~~ ~~buying a Labradoodle because they don't shed and because I like the word "Labradoodle"~~ important causes.

My wife is here tonight and I want to use this opportunity to say to her, "~~I'm leaving you.~~" "I love you." Without her constant ~~bitching~~ support, this book could never have been written. So, to you ~~Marsha~~ Martha (NOTE: double-check wife's name), "Thank you."

And to my children, Suri and Maddox, I hope this award helps you understand why Daddy spent so much time ~~drinking~~ working in his office when you wanted me to play. Do you remember what I used to tell you? "Daddy can't play right now because he's a genius." Now you have proof. So while it's true that other kids' daddies volunteer to coach Little League and help with ballet recitals, I want you two to always remember that those daddies didn't win important literary prizes—I did. Plus, a lot of important writers were horrible to their children. Look it up.

In conclusion, I want to thank all of my friends, colleagues, and ~~lovers~~ acquaintances here tonight. Each of you, in some small way, contributed to the creation of this ~~super awesome~~

humble little book. Each of you shares this prize with me. Not literally, of course, because that would necessitate me cutting up the award into tiny little pieces.

~~In your face, losers!~~

Thank you and good night.

Acknowledgments

FIRST of all, I would like to acknowledge that I have a terrible sense of direction. Whether I am on the road or on the couch, I rarely know where I am, and never know where I am going. Special thanks to the people who try to point me in the right direction: my editor Tricia Boczkowski, Ted Schachter, Kevin Stolper, Jay Gassner, Mike Mori, everybody in the New Group, Elijah, Ruth, and, of course, Martha.

About the Author

MICHAEL IAN BLACK has starred in many television series and films including *Stella*, *The State*, *Wet Hot American Summer*, *Viva Variety*, VH1's *I Love the . . .* series, and NBC's *Ed*. He wrote the screenplay for *Run, Fatboy, Run*, and wrote and directed the film *Wedding Daze*. Michael is also a popular stand-up comedian and world-champion poker player (not true). He lives in Connecticut with his wife and their two kids. His first children's book, *Chicken Cheeks*, was realeased in January 2009. His latest project is *Michael and Michael Have Issues*, a comedy series premiering in July 2009 on Comedy Central.